Among the Ashes

Among the Ashes

On Death, Grief, and Hope

WILLIAM J. ABRAHAM

William B. Eerdmans Publishing Company

Grand Rapids, Michigan

Wm. B. Eerdmans Publishing Co.
2140 Oak Industrial Drive NE, Grand Rapids, Michigan 49505
www.eerdmans.com

Published 2017
Printed in the United States of America

26 25 24 23 22 21 20 19 18 17   1 2 3 4 5 6 7 8 9 10

ISBN 978-0-8028-7528-0

Library of Congress Cataloging-in-Publication Data

Names: Abraham, William J. (William James), 1947– author.
Title: Among the ashes : on death, grief, and hope / William J. Abraham.
Description: Grand Rapids : Eerdmans Publishing Co., 2017. |
    Includes bibliographical references and index.
Identifiers: LCCN 2017018929 | ISBN 9780802875280
    (hardcover : alk. paper)
Subjects: LCSH: Death—Religious aspects—Christianity. | Grief—Religious
    aspects—Christianity. | Future life—Christianity. | Theodicy. | Hope—
    Religious aspects—Christianity. | Abraham, Timothy Fletcher, –2013.
Classification: LCC BT825 .A27 2017 | DDC 236/.1—dc23
    LC record available at https://lccn.loc.gov/2017018929

Unless otherwise noted, Scripture quotations are from the New Revised Standard Version of the Bible, copyright © 1989 by the Division of Christian Ed-
ucation of the National Council of the Churches of Christ in the U.S.A., and
used by permission.

In memoriam

Timothy Fletcher Abraham

May his memory be eternal

Contents

Foreword

William J. Abraham, gifted theologian and philosopher of religion, personal friend of mine, is well-versed in the literature on theodicy, that is, attempts to explain why, given who God is, there is evil in the world. He endorses the enterprise. Though he judges that no theodicy has succeeded in achieving the sought-for explanation—"there is no persuasive theological rationale for much of the suffering we have to endure"—he thinks many of them do illuminate various dimensions of Christian conviction. In the course of his discussion in this book he analyzes a few recent theodicies, highlighting those dimensions of Christian conviction that they illuminate and explaining why, in his judgment, they nonetheless do not explain why God allows evil.

On June 4, 2013, his adult son Timothy died unexpectedly, and Abraham was cast into deep grief. "To lose Timothy was to fall precipitously into a deep black hole. It was a hole of darkness, numbness, despair, and waves of excruciating pain." In this hole of darkness Abraham "found every philosophical or theological move utterly empty in wrestling with the problem of the loss of [his] son. The bottom line is that [he] wanted Timothy back.... Nothing by way of comment or explanation brought comfort, relief, or intellectual peace."

Why was that? "If these philosophical and theological proposals developed in theodicy are cogent, given that I can readily entertain them, surely they ought to have made a difference to my grieving and my terrible sense of loss. The reality is that they made no difference; on the contrary, entertaining them would have been entirely hollow and they would have come across as inappropriate or vacuous."

Might it be that his inability to entertain any theodicy in his grief showed that "the whole idea of theodicy [is] a snare and a delusion," as some claim? Abraham dismisses the suggestion. In no way does the death of his son undercut his judgment that theodicies do illuminate certain dimensions of Christian conviction. He writes, "I think our work on theodicy should remain intact and should be subject to renewal and development."

Might it then be, as others have suggested, that what is needed by those in grief is pastoral counseling rather than theological and philosophical reflections? Was it words that console that he needed, rather than reflections that purport to explain?

Abraham rejects this suggestion as well. He could no more think about his situation along pastoral lines than he could along theological and philosophical lines. He could not think about it at all. He found himself incapable of reasoning about his son's death and his own grief in any sustained way. "The effort to distinguish the pastoral from the philosophical and the more radical effort to reject work in theodicy both fail because they do not recognize or take seriously enough the significance" of what happens in grief. "What happens in this instance is the breakdown of our normal cognitive capacities. The darkness has snuffed out the light by which we engage in reason insofar as it relates to the excruciating loss involved."

The opening chapter of *Among the Ashes* is an in-depth consideration of this stark analysis. Though theodicies are relevant to the death of a child, and pastoral considerations relevant to the person in grief, the person in grief is incapable of entertaining those. "In this experience we are at a loss for words; we are reduced to rest and silence; we cannot say anything positive; the mystery involved is ineradicable. . . . Words fail us; we are too traumatized to speak; we simply have to sit or walk around or hold our heads in our hands and live with our piercing pain, our tears, our sobs, and our silences. We have to do what we can to find a way to get up and go on."

Eventually the intensity of his grief subsided and Abraham found himself once again capable of engaging in sustained reflection. Three topics then drew his attention, to each of which he devotes a chapter: first, the nature of life after death, as Scripture presents it, and the assurance and hope of Christians that they, and the ones they love, will experience such life; second, emulating Job in living with assurance and hope but without explanation; and third, the bearing of Christ's death on our death.

This is a deeply honest book. Abraham does not shirk from saying that in his grief he could not reason about the death of his son or about his grief. He does not shirk from saying that we have no theological explanation for the untimely death of children. He does not shirk from saying that, though we live without explanations, we nonetheless have ground for hope. Readers will find this honesty refreshing and consoling. It captures their experience, and it gives them permission to set aside pious talk and voice their own grief.

NICHOLAS WOLTERSTORFF

Preface

This little book began life on the arrival of a kind invitation to give the Trinity Lectures at Trinity Theological College, Singapore, in 2015. I knew immediately the topic that I wanted to pursue. As the initial chapter makes clear, dramatic events in my own life were the precipitating cause. In addition, I have for long been convinced that the topic of death is not one to be shunned because of its sobering nature but one that cuts to the heart of what we believe. So I offer here my ruminations on some central issues that surely deserve our attention. Even so, I do not for a moment think that it can amount to any kind of comprehensive treatment of the full range of issues that need to be explored. Thus I do not touch, for example, on the whole topic of purgatory, a theme that has been taken up in bold new ways by some contemporary theologians and philosophers. I do not find their arguments at all persuasive. Among other things, I think that the theme of purgatory distracts from the marvel of what God has promised us in the gospel and underestimates the amazing power of God made manifest in the life of Christ and in Christian conversion. Even so, much more could have been written to fill out the network of issues that should detain us here.

I have made a couple of changes from the text of the lectures as they were originally given. I have restructured the material in the chapter on assurance and hope; the original ordering made too much of the technical issues involved and overshadowed the thrust of what I wanted to argue. I have also added a chapter on the relation between death and the death of Christ. My efforts to tackle this difficult issue failed at the first attempt; I am now satisfied that I have made sufficient progress to publish my initial ruminations on this very demanding topic.

It was a great honor to be invited to give the Trinity Lectures. Singapore is an extraordinary place politically and religiously. The Christian community there is a tonic in terms of its Christian depth and its intellectual fecundity. Meeting with the faculty at Trinity Theological College and engaging the students and laity who attended the lectures was a breath of fresh air. I want to thank especially Dr. Roland Chia, who first contacted me and who worked through all the details to make my visit possible. The principal, Rev. Dr. Ngoei Foong Nghian, was a perfect host. The future of theology is in good hands in Singapore; it was a great joy to eavesdrop on their conversations. I thank them and the many friends that I have in Singapore for their magnificent hospitality.

CHAPTER 1

Death, Grief, and the Problem of Evil

O n Monday, June 4, 2013, at precisely 11:16 p.m., my beloved son Timothy died in Baylor Hospital in Dallas at
the age of forty-two.

Nine days earlier I had just spent a delightful evening
with some academic friends in a home close to St. Andrews
University in Scotland, working on the literary legacy of
Professor Basil Mitchell, my supervisor during my studies at
Oxford. Basil, who had become a close friend over the years,
had died about a year earlier at the age of ninety-two; so he
was very much on my mind over the preceding year and even
more so as I traveled to secure various letters and papers of
his in England and Scotland. At 11:30 in the evening I got
the kind of call that every parent dreads. Shaun, my younger
son, called to tell me that earlier that afternoon Timothy had
gone to the doctor and was then rushed to the hospital. While
Shaun had gone home to get Muriel, his mother, to bring her
to the hospital, Timothy had suffered the complete collapse
of his vital organs. We found out later that the precipitating cause was hepatitis. It was extremely fortunate that the

catastrophic collapse had occurred while he was at Baylor Hospital; the full resources of the hospital were immediately deployed and they were able to save him, at least in the short term. His death, nine days later, was to all of us in the family unexpected; we were not prepared for it.

His younger sister, Siobhan, who was traveling in France, got a similar phone call to the one that I got in Scotland. The message was urgent. We were both to get back as soon as possible, for the prospects of survival were slim. Siobhan made it back four hours ahead of me two days later. To say that those two days were a nightmare would be a gross understatement. The swing from faint hope to deep anguish and despair ripped through every fiber of my existence as I drove with a friend from St. Andrews to Manchester, spent a night there, and then flew back home to Dallas via Chicago. The thought of never again hearing Timothy climb the stairs and of never seeing him again put his head around the corner of the doorway was excruciating. He was a confirmed and happy Irish bachelor who, following our native traditions, lived at home. I could see the future ahead as nothing but bleak and miserable without him in our lives. While I clung to every scrap of information on my frequent calls back home to Shaun to find out what was happening, deep down I had already begun to compose in my mind the testimony to Timothy that I was determined to make publicly should the worst scenario arise. Aside from continual prayer for healing (indeed for a miracle of healing) my last-resort prayer was that Timothy would still be alive when I got back. When this was answered, my next prayer was that at some stage he would wake up from the induced coma and I could tell him how much I loved him. That prayer too was answered; in retrospect the answer to that prayer was and is an incredible gift.

Yet the bigger issue remains: despite a massive outpouring of prayer, my beloved Timothy was not healed. Our own personal and family prayers for healing were accompanied by prayers across the world as news spread through Facebook, email, phone calls, and word of mouth. I do not want to single out one group of people, for the outpouring came from family, friends, colleagues in ministry, the clergy and laity of our local church, faculty colleagues, faraway acquaintances, and a host of folk who wrote tender letters of condolences afterwards. Yet the one very moving response by way of prayer came from a network of churches in Nepal with whom I have worked in mission over the last ten years. I got one email showing a picture of a large group of children holding a prayer service where Timothy's picture was eventually displayed as a way to bring focus to their intercession. In my own case I engaged in my own personal prayer for healing, at one point going to Vespers in the local Orthodox cathedral with Shaun, where I could immerse myself in the liturgy for the season of Pentecost for over half an hour.

The end came on Monday, June 4. As the days wore on we could see that there was no turnaround on the crucial benchmarks that the medical team had in place as a sign of recovery. As a family we consulted together from the beginning; we worked out a consensus that in the end I would make the final decision as to whether we would continue life-support. I met with the leader of the medical team around four o'clock in the afternoon and gave permission to switch off the life-support systems. We gathered together as a family at six o'clock to remove all forms of medical assistance except those normally retained to ensure the alleviation of acute pain. We stood together at his bedside for the five remaining hours of his life. The love and care of Muriel and

Siobhan in those final hours were astonishing; they talked him through to the other side; the pain for Shaun and me was virtually unbearable, so there was little we could say or do, but we made it through as best we could. We traveled home in silence in the aftermath, leaving one car in the hospital car park so that we could be together.

The literature on grief uses all sorts of images to capture the suffering that occurs on occasions like this. A favorite one is the loss of a limb. Mine is equally simple: to lose Timothy was to fall precipitously into a deep black hole. It was a hole of darkness, numbness, despair, and waves of excruciating pain. I had lost a friend, a counselor, a soulmate, a fellow-traveler, a spiritual companion, and a conversation partner; and, above all else, I had lost my firstborn son. Everything was touched in one way or another. The family could never be the same again, not just on this or that special occasion but forever. Our person-relative grief would spill over into each other's grief, reaching as far as our extended families in Ireland. My youngest brother, Ivan, arranged to have a prayer service at home in Ireland while we were conducting the funeral in Dallas; Timothy's cousins on his mother's side of the family held a short vigil at his grandparents' grave at the same time. My loss and grief began to seep into everything I did, from my daily routines to a new orientation in my teaching and a new perspective on my research and writing. I had achieved a new identity; I was now a father who had lost a son. I have kept a journal to chart developments and to house various bits and pieces of advice and memorabilia.

What I have just articulated is a small part of the impact of what happens when the healing we hoped and prayed for does not come. Two of my prayers were indeed answered.

I was able to see Timothy before he died; and I was able to tell him that I loved him when he became intermittently conscious. Moreover, I count it a wonderful providence that I could be with him when he died; the memory of those last hours will live with me forever, I suspect. However, the hoped-for and prayed-for healing did not come.

Later I came across a prayer by Charles Wesley on the eve of the death of his firstborn son, John, who died on January 7, 1754. He died of smallpox, while his mother survived. This poem captures much of what I prayed for during those terrible nine days of initial agony, when we still sought the face of God for Timothy's survival and healing.

God of love, incline thine ear,
Hear a cry of grief and fear,
Hear an anxious Parent's cry,
Help, before my Isaac die.

All my comfort in distress,
All my earthly happiness,
Spare him still, the precious Loan;
Is he not my only Son?

Whom I did from Thee obtain
Must I give him back again?
Can I with the blessing part?
Lord, Thou know'st a Mother's heart:

All its passionate excess.
All its yearning tenderness,
Nature's soft infirmity,
Is it not a drop from Thee?

For Thy own compassion's sake,
Give me then my Darling back
Rais'd as from the dead, to praise,
Love, and serve Thee all his days.

Speak, and at Thy powerful word,
Lo, the witness to his Lord,
Monument of grace divine,
Isaac lives, for ever Thine![1]

I have described my experience as falling into a black hole. What is paradoxical about that experience is that everything around it was marked by an abundance of providence. I have already mentioned that both Siobhan and I were able to get back from Europe on time. We had those final but difficult nine days with Timothy. That in turn gave us time to put things in order if we had to face the worst-case scenario, so that when the end came we were prepared. In the period before the funeral we called in a plumber to do some work on the home; when he discovered what we were going through he waived the costs and refused to change his mind when I tried to pay. The amount of care, not to speak of expenditure, provided by some of the best of the best in medical expertise at Baylor was amazing. The help I got from my dean and from colleagues was extraordinary. The care that was lavished upon us by our local church was tangible without being suffocating. Even the send-off at the funeral was everything we could have wanted. I was able to take Timothy's ashes on a kind of final farewell around the university he loved and where he had found his feet intellectually before I delivered them for overnight keeping at the church. Friends came in from afar to provide comfort and reassurance. I was given the strength to deliver a personal tribute to Timothy. Dean William Lawrence provided everything one could wish in terms of the liturgy and preaching at the funeral itself. The family held together through the crisis and is now closer than ever (think of the families torn apart by a crisis like this). Siobhan was between jobs and thus was able to stay for three whole months in Dallas to help us work things through and set Timothy's affairs in order.

Consider this further development. Timothy was not a churchy person; he could not stand pious claptrap; but he was a believer and showed it in his own inimitable ways. We decided that in lieu of flowers we should open a fund for the one area where he had shown an interest to help, namely the mission work in Nepal that is supported through Oasis International Ministries. The folk in Nepal prayed about what to do with the money collected and they decided to build a church in his honor outside Kathmandu. Normally it takes about $5,000 to $6,000 to build a church in Nepal. Two weeks ago we sent somewhat more than $26,000 to buy a significant block of land for a very special church outside Kathmandu, with a view of the mountains where in time there will also be a retreat center. Another $10,000 is needed to build the church and begin the bigger project; I am confident the funding will arrive in God's good time. I can only say that Timothy would get a real kick out of this whole project; I can well imagine the grin, the look in his eye, and then the wit that would readily pour forth from his lively mind and articulate lips. The last thing in the world he would have expected is a church and retreat center built in his honor outside Kathmandu in Nepal.

So the healing I hoped for did not come. Instead we got death and grief and a black hole of darkness surrounded paradoxically by providence. In speaking as I do, I am working from below and out from my own experience. Other cases, perhaps the one you are struggling with, would require a very different analysis and commentary. In the case before us, we can readily work up a taxonomy of challenges. Let me flag three initial challenges briefly and then look at one other longstanding issue in more detail.[2]

Consider, first, the ordinary psychological challenges of guilt, anxiety, disorientation, pain, and loss. The obvious antidote is pastoral care, talking things through in the family, cultivating commonsense survival skills, and, where needed, effective grief counseling at a professional level.

Consider, second, the question of unanswered prayer. Why did the Lord not grant our request for healing? Here the answer is simple: God does indeed know best. Our perspective and range of information is limited. To submit to the will of God is utterly apt and decisively correct. For me it makes no intellectual or theological sense whatsoever to get mad or angry at God. Of course, emotionally and psychologically it makes sense when we get angry at God in these circumstances. However, it makes no coherent or intellectual sense given what I believe about God; and I have not had the slightest temptation to do so. God's speech to Job out of the whirlwind says all that needs to be said on this score from a theological point of view. I will return to this later in the penultimate chapter.

Consider, third, the challenge of understanding death theologically. I can understand how death in the long haul of the Christian tradition has been cast as an enemy; it is the last enemy, an enemy defeated by Christ's resurrection, which is in turn a preview of the general resurrection to come, where death and sin will finally be defeated. However, it is not easy to know how to unpack the idea of death as an enemy. Generally the way to unpack this has been to provide a reading of Genesis 3 and of Paul that sees death in physical terms and to cast death as a consequence of sin or as punishment of ancestral sin. Alternatively, the issue has been cast not in terms of physical death but of spiritual death; so that death as an enemy is interpreted in terms of death as a spiritual death and of sin being the cause of our fear of death as a physical phenomenon. So the cultivation of a good death (a prominent theme in early Methodism and in the *ars moriendi* tradition) is a matter of dealing with the fear of death in terms of repentance, confession, meditation, the reliance on the sacramental practice of the church, and the like. So while we do not for a moment understate the significance of the physical death of our Lord as it actually happened contingently in history, we can see the defeat of death in terms of new life in the Spirit here and now and then in terms of a death marked by patience, repentance, and humble, hopeful assurance, all generated by grace.

So much for noting three obvious challenges. Now let me tackle another one in some detail. By far the most obvious challenge is the challenge posed by theodicy. Given that God is good and almighty, how come our prayers for healing are not always answered? If God is good, God will be motivated to heal; if God is almighty, God has the capacity to heal. So how come our prayers for healing are given a negative answer? Or if this is too abstract, how come God heals in some cases and not in this one? These are not clever or trick exam questions; they are entirely genuine. As we proceed to deal with this standard worry about the internal coherence of the Christian faith, let me set aside the temptation to deal with this question by saying that while there was no physi-

cal healing there was in fact a higher healing. I know what
this means, but it will not suffice as an answer to my query
because in an obvious sense there was no healing at all. Let
me also lay aside the temptation to account for unanswered
prayer by saying that we did not pray with sufficient faith. No
doubt this may be true, but in this instance there was surely
enough faith somewhere, not least among those children in
Nepal. So I want to take a further look at the impact of my
experience on what to do with the question of theodicy.

Notice that the challenge becomes more acute given
that I believe in miracles and that I am prepared to pray for a
miracle. These assumptions (although these are not the only
assumptions) govern my own robust commitment to the
ministry of healing. Of course, if Timothy had been healed
by natural means, I would have immediately thanked God
for his providence, for in a broad sense we readily acknowledge that God works through natural and human means.
However, it is theologically reductionist and epistemically
skeptical to confine God to these means to bring about a
healing. If one believes in not just the possibility but the past
actuality of direct divine healing, then the problem is more
acute than it is for those forms of liberal Protestantism that
set limits to the action of God.[3] God could have intervened
and acted directly in answer to prayer; and God did not do
so. Given *this* construal of divine power, coupled with divine
goodness, then the issue of theodicy becomes even more
acute than it is for the generic theist, or for the liberal Protestant or for the dispensationalist evangelical.[4]

One standard angle of vision on this is that we should
distinguish between the philosophical questions in and
around theodicy from the more pastoral or spiritual problems that one has to deal with, say, on the loss of a loved one.

Given the potential psychological agony, questions of theodicy should be set aside until one regains one's equilibrium. At the philosophical level, then, one can deploy all the conventional moves, that is, the free will defense, the moral and spiritual growth defense, and the skeptical theistic defense. In the last instance one makes the persuasive move (deployed already above in relation to unanswered prayer) that in this life we simply cannot see all that God sees and must leave things in his good hands. If one adds in, as I would, the crucial place of divine providence in life, and the even more crucial place of divine revelation in Israel and in Jesus Christ, then in fact I am more than ready to defend both the almighty power of God and the unsurpassed goodness of God as entirely compatible with the experience I have been through. In other words, the lack of healing in this instance does not begin to count, all things considered, as a defeater to the central claims of the Christian faith. Moreover, I insisted on saying this even in the midst of the darkness that enveloped me.

What I suspect is that this experience of darkness may challenge the sharp distinction between pastoral and philosophical considerations, a distinction that suggests we shelve issues of theodicy until the grief is over. I sense no need to shelve the issues of theodicy. The point I initially want to make can be put this way: I know all the standard moves in theodicy and even endorse a robust and integrated set of those moves; I do not sense that these are somehow irrelevant to my situation; what I find is that they are intellectually incapable of doing any work in my life. What is at issue is that I found every philosophical or theological move utterly empty in wrestling with the problem of the loss of my son. The bottom line is that I wanted Timothy back here; I wanted him back even if I had to spend the rest of my own life tending to his needs. Nothing by way of comment or explanation brought comfort, relief, or intellectual peace. If these philosophical and theological proposals developed in theodicy are cogent, given that I can readily entertain them, surely they ought to have made a difference to my grieving and my terrible sense of loss. The reality is that they made no difference; on the contrary, entertaining them would have been entirely hollow and they would have come across as inappropriate or vacuous. Yet if they were cogent, and I think they indeed are, this should not have been the case. For an intelligent, rational agent, in all other circumstances considerations as persuasive as these should and would be registered, and appropriate emotional and spiritual adjustments should and would then have been made.

This gap between reflective theory and experience is surely one reason why there is now a vast literature attacking, if not ridiculing, the whole idea of theodicy as a snare and a delusion. If rational considerations fail so abysmally in this case, then the game is up. We should treat this dead-end as a *reductio ad absurdum* of the whole effort to find a theodicy in either its negative or positive forms. The experience of unanswered prayer as represented by the absence of divine healing undercuts in the depths of one's heart and soul the whole effort to find a defense of God or to find a positive account as to why God should not have healed my son. One can ratchet up the scale of this by multiplying the level of evil to include the kind of horrendous moral and natural evils that have been discussed of late in the literature. Every effort to develop a defensive or positive theodicy collapses within the experience of darkness in these very difficult cases. So the solution, some propose, is to abandon the project. One simply insists that faith and reason are incompatible; and one proceeds to live by faith with integrity and finesse. Authenticity and integrity should be retained whatever the intellectual sacrifices that have to be made.

I am not at all convinced that this is the right inference to draw from my observations on the intellectual impotency of theodicy in the face of deep suffering. I think our work on theodicy should remain intact and should be subject to renewal and development. Consequently, I want to look deeper into the experience involved and provide another perspective on the inadequacy of the pastoral/philosophical distinction. More to the point, I shall seek to explain why the motivation behind the rejection of theodicy is not persuasive once one comes to understand what is happening in the experience of loss I have already described.

The way forward at this stage is to return to my earlier description and note something important about its mode and content. There are good and bad ways for death to happen. Or, if that is too strong, there are bad ways to die and there are worse ways to die. For me Timothy's death was tragic. It could have been prevented; and it cut him down just at the point where he was really getting his life together and beginning to fulfill his dreams professionally. Thinking abstractly about death, I can think of many worse ways to die. Many people, including children, die absolutely horrendous deaths; to see this listen to the daily news, or read the literature of the Gulag, or attend to the lives of the martyrs. However, my experience of Timothy's death took the family and me across a threshold of grief and agony where you simply hit rock bottom. The experience speaks for itself as the worst that one will ever have to face. There is nothing below it; it is darkness all the way down. The subjective experience in all its brutality does not allow for an objective account that can trump it in the scale of misery and pain. The first-person perspective of darkness overrides considerations that arise from a third-person perspective of light.

Ordinary people understand this, and it is the chief reason why they eschew and even cringe at pious nonsense. They simply stand with you as best they can as a nonanxious presence and they reach out to help as best they can. Just as I wanted to give my own life in exchange for Timothy's so he could live and fulfill his dreams, so sensitive friends wanted to do anything in their power to help the family and me get through the agony. Folk readily made the following remarks: "This shouldn't be. It is out of order that a father should bury a son; it should be the other way round." "I will not even try to understand what you are going through right now because words would fail me." "I have no idea what you are going through because I can only begin to imagine what it is like. I do not know what it is like."

Let's call an experience like this apophatic; and let's call any effort to make sense of the experience theologically cataphatic. By the apophatic I simply mean, following ancient usage as applied to God, that in this experience we are at a loss for words; we are reduced to rest and silence; we cannot say anything positive; the mystery involved is ineradicable. By the cataphatic I mean here any attempt to describe and explain in positive theological terms what is happening. In this experience the cataphatic is strictly in abeyance; it is set aside. Words fail us; we are too traumatized to speak; we simply have to sit or walk around or hold our heads in our hands and live with our piercing pain, our tears, our sobs, and our silences. We have to do what we can to find a way to

get up and go on, to secure strategies of survival and nego-
tiation when speech itself fails us.

This apophatic experience in turn colors everything we
say in the face of the intellectual challenges of death in the
wake of persistent and concerted intercessory prayer for
healing. In this situation any philosophical or theological
discourse from a third-person perspective fails. To be told
that God permits it for his good purposes, or that Timothy
is now in the hands of his Savior, or that good things will
come out of this suffering, or that we walk by faith and not
by sight, has no purchase on us intellectually. These claims
in my judgment are all true; I even believe, contrary to contemporary theological indifference and skepticism, that they
constitute knowledge and have made the case for that elsewhere. However, any cataphatic claim has no purchase in
the presence of the apophatic experience I am describing.

The effort to distinguish the pastoral from the philosophical and the more radical effort to reject work in theodicy both fail because they do not recognize or take seriously
enough the significance of the apophatic nature of our experience as manifested in deep grief and loss. What happens
in this instance is the breakdown of our normal cognitive
capacities. The darkness has snuffed out the light by which
we engage in reason insofar as it relates to the excruciating
loss involved.[5]

Think of it this way. Human agents are extraordinarily
sensitive truth-detecting organisms. We have sense organs
that register what is happening around us in sight, hearing,
taste, smell, and touch. We have intricate memories that recall what happened to us in the recent and distant past. We
have a moral sense that distinguishes good from evil; and we
have a social sense that picks up what is happening around

us, say, in a meeting. We have an aesthetic sense that picks up, say, the beauty of a piece of music; and we have a spiritual sense for discerning holiness and detecting the presence and activity of God in the world, in Christ, and in the depths of our own hearts and consciences. With these and other warrants in place we have the capacity to construct truthful accounts of events, of complex experiences, of the world around us, and of the world of creation and redemption. For the most part these accounts are fallible and corrigible; they are also reliable and can be enriched by further experience and reflection, both on our own and in community. The core idea here is the notion captured in externalist and proper function accounts of epistemology that highlight the place of native capacities and powers in developing accurate theories about ourselves, about the world, about God, and about all that God has done in creation and redemption. My way of putting it is quite simple: we are extraordinarily sensitive truth-detecting organisms made by God with amazing cognitive capacities and powers.

What happens in deep grief of the sort I am seeking to describe is that our genuine but fragile capacities are overwhelmed; they can only deliver what emerges as a first-person perspective. Considerations at the level of third-person perspectives fail to register; they become at best empty and hollow; at worst they are insensitive and otiose. We cease to operate in our normal cognitive environment, and we face a radical breakdown of our normal intellectual capacities, powers, and skills. The correct lesson to be learned from this observation is that we should be wary of the inferences we draw about the relation between first- and third-person perspectives in the experience of deep loss. Both the rejection of theodicy and the effort to defend theodicy by drawing a distinction between the pastoral and the philosophical are efforts to draw a hasty and immediate inference from the significance of trauma. I think the appropriate inference to draw is that our cognitive capacities, powers, and skills have lost their moorings. The anti-theodicist argues that because explanations fail when we deal with deep grief we should reject any effort at theodicy. This is crucial in the motivation to reject theodicies of any kind. The theodicist says that, given the grief, we should not expect theodicy to speak in any meaningful way to people who have just suffered the loss of a loved one. Given these two options, the latter is certainly closer to the right inference; but the theodicist's move lacks any explanatory power; it fails to see why grief has the effect that it does. To get to that level, we have to go one step further and come to terms with a full-scale epistemology that gives pride of place to the human agent in epistemology as a whole. The correct inference to draw is that we are operating in a radically abnormal epistemic environment; thus our normal third-person perspectives generally fail to register.

However, the defender of theodicy who draws a distinction between pastoral and philosophical considerations is surely on to something of enormous significance. I shall end my reflections by very brief commentary on what I think may be at issue or in the neighborhood of the issue. In cases where healing has been hoped for but does not come we do indeed need pastoral care. We might also add here that this means that when we engage in the ministry of healing we need to do so with confidence and yet with sensitivity and good sense. The relevant point to register, however, is that what we really need is plenteous divine grace. In a way we need grace for the healing of our hearts and minds; we need the restoration of our cognitive capacities and powers. Interestingly, it is surely inappropriate for such healing to take the form of an instant miracle. By its very nature, healing in this instance will necessarily take time, for a quick and instantaneous healing would call into question our love for Timothy. It is precisely because of our deep love that healing takes time. The healing grace we need characteristically does not come willy-nilly or in a vacuum; divine grace comes through means of grace. This is precisely why the church develops liturgical and other practices to help us; what is at issue is not just human care, itself a means of divine grace, but divine care, strength, energy, and healing mediated through personal and corporate practices.

The problem arises in an acute fashion after the funeral. On this score I have found my own tradition to be impoverished. I say this not by way of criticism but as a matter of fact. To address the problem I have had to develop my own fragile means of grace to survive and work my way through to a healthy future. On this front my network of practices was quite simple. I borrowed from the Jewish tradition the idea of taking a year to grieve in an intentional way. Across that year I pledged to do the following. Every weekend when I was in town, before I taught my first class in my local church, I would visit the columbarium where Timothy's ashes rest, and hold my hand as close as I could to the urn that contains his mortal remains. I remembered him and my love for him explicitly. Every day when my mind wandered to him in thought, I paused and stayed with my thoughts. At times I would deliberately just sit and think about him and how much he meant to me. Every day I recited from memory the simple, uncomplicated prayer for the dead that can be found in any collection of Eastern Orthodox prayers.

O God of spirits and of all flesh, Who hast trampled down death and overthrown the Devil, and given life to Thy world, do Thou, the same Lord, give rest to the souls of Thy departed servants in a place of brightness, a place of refreshment, a place of repose, where all sickness, sighing, and sorrow have fled away. Pardon every transgression which they have committed, whether by word or deed or thought. For Thou art a good God and lovest mankind; because there is no man who lives yet does not sin, for Thou only art without sin, Thy righteousness is to all eternity, and Thy word is truth. For Thou art the Resurrection, the Life, and the Repose of Thy servants who have fallen asleep, O Christ our God, and unto Thee we ascribe glory, together with Thy Father, who is from everlasting, and Thine all-holy, good, and life-creating Spirit, now and ever unto ages of ages. Amen.

Every time I participated in the Lord's Supper I would think of him and of all who gather in the church triumphant. I kept a notebook and when appropriate I recorded my own journey of grief and saved this or that scrap of hymnody or commentary that I found helpful. I did this for a year. Then, on the first anniversary of his death I planned to find some way to mark that day both as an end-point and a new beginning. I was given a *Jahrzeit* candle by a Jewish friend; it burns for exactly twenty-four hours. I could not, however, make the transition on the anniversary of his death. At that point I knew I was in trouble. So I moved the transition to the anniversary of his funeral and was able at that point to turn a new page in my life and my grief.

I was partly helped in all this by realizing that Timothy himself would have fully endorsed this move. Since then I continue to hold vigil on special days like his birthday. And I continue to visit his grave on a regular basis.

I noted earlier that compared to other traditions our tradition is somewhat impoverished. If I am right about this, then the impoverishment lies on our end, not on the divine end represented by the abundant reserves of divine grace. In seeking to renew the riches of divine promise and energy available for healing, we should not stop short and forget the resources available for lament when healing does not take place as we had hoped. I finish with one such resource that I have recorded in my journal and carried around in my pocket. It is a poem from Charles Wesley on the occasion of the death of his firstborn son. Let me conclude by quoting three verses from a total of six.

> Mine earthly happiness is fled,
>   His mother's joy, his father's hope,
> (O had I dy'd in *Isaac's* stead)
>   He should have liv'd, my age's prop,
> He *should* have closed his father's eyes,
>   And followed me to paradise.

> But hath not heaven, who first bestow'd,
>   A right to take His gifts away?
> I bow me to the sovereign God,
>   Who snatched him from the evil day!
> Yet nature will repeat her moan,
>   And fondly cry, "My son, my son!"

> From us, as we from him, secure,
>   Caught to his heavenly Father's breast,
> He waits, till we the bliss insure,

From all these stormy sorrows rest,
And see him with our Angel stand,
    To waft, and welcome us to land.

Even as he laments the death of his son, Charles Wesley displays here his characteristic conviction that there is indeed a life beyond death. In the next chapter I will take up what we should believe positively about life after death for those who die in Christ and explore why we believe this to be the case.

CHAPTER 2

Life after Death, Divine Revelation, and Reason

One of the deep effects of the grief that ensues on the death of a loved one—in my case, the death of my beloved son Timothy—is that one's cognitive capacities are simply overwhelmed. So much so that beliefs and convictions that common sense would say should make a difference fail to do so. This does not mean that grieving as a Christian will not have a different phenomenology from that of the unbeliever. As Paul notes, we do not grieve like certain pagans may do, that is, without hope. However, we cannot pretend that this overrides what I described as entering a black hole where one's convictions fail to register in the sense that they fail to alleviate the depth of one's grief in the loss, say, of a beloved son. This was certainly my case; and I am certain from informal testimony that this is also the case for others. What is at issue is something entirely normal rather than pathological.

It was this observation that led me to go beyond the debate within philosophy and theology on what to do with the problem of evil understood as a debate between fideism and theodicy. Consider these alternatives as posing these two contrasting options. Should we read the situation as one that calls into question every effort to make sense of the experience in terms of seeking theological explanations for what happened? In taking this option, we operate entirely by faith alone; reason is empty and ineffective. Or should we distinguish between pastoral and philosophical treatments of grief and insist that there is a time and place for reflection on why God, by not answering our prayers for healing, at the very least permitted what happened? If choosing this option, we live in the short term by faith, but in the long term we explore the possibilities of explanation and reason. We enter here the dispute between those who attack and those who defend the whole idea of theodicy whether general or particular. I think that the fideist is right to draw attention to the deep effects of grief not just pastorally but intellectually, but she draws the wrong conclusion from her observation. Defenders of theodicy are in the main correct in their endeavors, but they miss the crucial epistemological significance of grief by reducing it initially to a mere pastoral problem. My goal in part is to remove the tension set up by the debate between fideists and theodicists by drawing the debate into the arena of epistemology. We have to add crucial epistemological data if we are to get beyond the stalemate.

A subsidiary aim in this book also seeks to bring to light and resolve a related tension that shows up in treatments of death, namely the tension between revelation and reason in thinking through the evidence for Christian claims about life after death. There are in fact three issues in place here. How do we understand the content of Christian teaching about life after death? What evidence should we deploy, if any, in order to underwrite our confidence in such teaching?

When we look for evidence, what kind of evidence is apt and relevant? The first of these three questions is logically prior to the second, even though we intuitively sense that they are intimately related. The third simply arises as we take up the second; we need not here determine logical or temporal priority. My working assumption is that we can get to the question of what counts as relevant evidence both materially and formally only after we lay out a relatively robust account of life after death. Here this issue can be introduced by asking this question: What minimally does the Christian faith teach about life after death in the arena of personal eschatology? Put differently, what is the canonical content of Christian claims about life after death?

I put the issue this way for at least two reasons. First, a lot of Christians are confused about what to believe about life after death. No doubt this stems in part from the skeptical orientation that we pick up in the West with our mother's milk. In part it stems from populist convictions that show up around funerals when we are told that those who have died have gone straight to heaven. So we need to clear up the confusion, which oscillates between skepticism and assured assertion. Second, without some sort of robust account of the content of Christian teaching about life after death, we are at a loss to know how to think through what counts as relevant evidence for such claims. The platitude to follow here is quite simple: the nature of the subject matter determines the nature of the evidence to be consulted.

How should we think of life after death? The topic in terms of classical eschatology can be identified as personal eschatology over against cosmic eschatology. To put it in street terms, we want to know what happens to us when we die, both in the short term and in the long term. By "us," I mean those who die in genuine faith in Jesus Christ as their Savior and Lord. I am deliberately leaving aside the debate about those who have never heard of Jesus of Nazareth and those who have rejected the claims of Christ on their lives. For our purposes what we need is a summary that is both meaty and minimal. I want to acknowledge that Christians have disagreed on certain elements in treatments of life after death. Thus they have disagreed, say, on the existence and nature of purgatory. I shall not be diffident about such disagreement, but I want to keep to an option that most would recognize as capturing crucial elements in their account of personal eschatology. Suppose we think of a minimal account as consisting of the following two elements. First, we survive our death by entering an intermediate state of rest and paradise without a body. Second, at the final return of Christ in glory we undergo a final judgment and are joined to a new resurrection body in a new creation and a new earth. It is these two claims that I want to take as the heart of the matter.

I am fully aware that these two claims presuppose the pivotal anthropological claim that human agents are best construed as embodied souls who survive the dissolution of their bodies. Sixty years ago this would have been considered heretical in many theological circles, especially among those who took any talk of souls as a denial of the biblical doctrine of essential embodiment and a fall into Greek doctrines of the immortality of the soul. This lingers on in Christian philosophical circles and in theological circles today and is sometimes supported by efforts to appeal to two disparate forms of argument. First, it is thought to conflict with the findings of neuroscience in that the latter is more or less seen as proving that human agents are essentially complex physical organisms. Second, it is often thought that this kind of metaphysical account of the human person represents a moral failure in that it has the tendency to undercut a robust commitment to the physical care of human beings by focusing on the care of the soul or focusing on the crucial priority of life in the world to come. I find the latter argument entirely specious in that it is contradicted by both logic and history. Logically, the care of human agents physically is easily secured by various elements in Christian theology that stand independently of the metaphysical vision of human agents I have enumerated. Historically, there are large numbers of Christians who believe in the priority of care of the soul over care of the body and yet who absolutely insist that we take care of human bodies by way of physical healing, relevant social services, and the like. The first argument deserves, however, a longer comment, albeit still brief and even dogmatic, because it touches on empirical considerations related to life after death that I shall take up later in the book. So I shall postpone my response to it till then.

It is important in thinking about this schematic account of personal eschatology not to confuse its brevity with its significance. While one can write the schema on a postcard, this does not apply to the amazing content that lies below the surface. Life after death is not just one more item in the course of our lives; it is a breakthrough of enormous proportions. Thus it signals that human agents are not just one more item in the evolution of life; we are creatures of earth who are destined for eternal glory. We are agents with extraordinary dignity and freedom whose lives and actions on this earth really do matter; we participate in a drama in which the parts we play prepare us for a fitting climax in the final victory of God over the world, the flesh, and the devil.

Within that drama we are the recipients of a salvation that begins here and now and will be consummated in the future.

That salvation was brought to us within human history in the person and work of the eternal Son of God who gave his life for our liberation from the guilt and penalty of sin by dying for us; that in turn opened up the possibility of genuine new creation through his extraordinary resurrection and the bestowal of the gift of the Holy Spirit. Thus the life to come is not a mere addendum, a happy accident that shows up as a matter of happenstance. It is the fulfillment of the promise of eternal life already bestowed upon us by faith and repentance ministered through the life and ministry of the church here and now. The down payment given to us by God in this life is consummated by the full payment of what God has promised and planned from the depths of eternity. Earlier generations represented by the *ars moriendi* tradition, the tradition of a good death, felt this keenly. They saw this life as a critical phase of a wider narrative that lifted its gaze above and beyond to behold the glory that lay ahead of them. One can catch the same sense of eager anticipation in many of the hymns of Charles Wesley (many of them end with entry into heaven); it shows up also in the network of marvelous (if at times sentimental) hymns developed in the North American gospel tradition.

If we think that looking to such a future is somehow a distraction or that it renders this life on earth insignificant, then we have failed to read our situation accurately. Students who know that they will have a set of final exams surely will use their time wisely to prepare for it throughout the course of their studies. If there is a glorious day up ahead for us, say, a wedding or the celebration of a special anniversary, we will not only be cheered by its prospects, we will take time to get ready for the great day up ahead. If I believe that I am moving to Romania for the last stretch of my life, I will not only learn the language; I will also change my current course of actions in anticipation of this significant change of circumstances. If this applies to mundane, this-worldly changes in our lives, how much more so does it apply to the prospects of eternal life beyond the grave? Consider what it will be to inhabit a universe where we shall meet our loved ones anew; where we shall encounter the saints and martyrs of old who have labored in God's vineyard across the generations; where all tears will be wiped from our eyes; where the days of oppression and brutality will be over once and for all; and where we shall enjoy an apt union with the triune God in a new and fitting environment.

For many, speaking like this is simply too good to be true. More generally, it can readily come across as a form of fantasy thinking. For many, it strains credibility to the limit. We are all aware, at least in Europe and North America, how this kind of robust vision of human existence and its destiny has become virtually obsolete in our public culture. We need not here take sides on the manifold debates about secularization to note that we live in a moral and intellectual universe where this whole way of thinking has become at best marginalized and at worst dismissed as poisonous and counterproductive. In working in systematic theology over the last twenty years in a world in Texas that has been saturated with Christianity, I find that current students are at a loss on what to say about personal eschatology. They readily retreat to platitudes about the life to come that are devoid of significant existential import. This may be an improvement on the network of theologians who have essentially abandoned any belief in personal survival, but it represents not just thin gruel but a real failure of intellectual nerve and imagination. They pounce on worries that reflection on life after death will be a distraction from transformative social action in this life. They turn with relief to theologies of liberation that enable them to change the subject and sally forth to change the world. For those who have lost a loved one and naturally ask searching theological questions about the life to come, this kind of response is both pastorally irresponsible and intellectually evasive.

Yet we cannot but have sympathy with the silence and embarrassment that talk of life after death naturally evokes. We surely experience the skeptical inclinations of our own hearts and minds. In my own life I became a relieved if immature atheist as a teenager after attending funerals in my native Ireland. The claims about life after death struck me as simply incredible. There was a massive gap between what I could see with my own eyes (people died and returned to dust and ashes) and what I heard heralded in the liturgy (we look to the resurrection of the dead). As far as I could see, folk simply died and that was the end of them. Below the surface I had come to embrace a simpleminded materialism: human agents are in the end simply forms of material reality. The very idea of any kind of survival, least of all survival of the soul, made no coherent sense to me. Much of my intellectual life has been taken up with working my way out of this entirely secular orientation into the full canonical riches of the Christian tradition, a journey I expect to continue for the rest of my life.

In this skeptical context there can be no evading the need to answer the question: If this is what Christians minimally believe, what grounds if any do they offer in support of the astonishing claims that they advance? And in the neighborhood of this question there is the obvious second-order, epistemological question: What kinds of considerations are relevant if we want to pursue this question aptly? The two in fact are logically connected, for decisions about relevant material evidence depend on decisions about what counts as relevant and apt data; and the case applies vice versa.

We can make immediate headway by noting what kind of claim we have before us. It is essentially a theological claim about divine action and intention. It is a proposal about the agency of God with respect to the future of those of his creatures who are made in his image, redeemed by the precious blood of his Son, and brought to new life through the working of the Holy Spirit. It is natural of course to frame the issue initially as a set of questions about human agents. Do human agents survive their physical dissolution? Will we see our loved ones again in the world to come? Will I survive my own death? We can and do ask these questions without any reference to divine creation, redemption, and consummation; ordinary folk do it all the time. Moreover, as we shall see, ordinary folk are interested in securing relevant data to answer these questions. However, these are not initially the questions that the mature Christian believer should ask. The issue has to be framed as a set of theological questions about God's intentions and plans for human agents. Has God designed and created us in such a way so as to secure our survival in a life to come? Has God created us to live out our physical existence and that is the end of us? Does divine redemption of us as sinners and wayward creatures apply merely to our salvation in this world or does it include future consummation in a life to come?

Once we reframe the issues in this way, then two consequences immediately follow.

First, the debate is not about the immortality of the soul as found, say, in Greek philosophy. To put the issue this way is to make it a metaphysical debate about the nature of the soul and completely miss what is at stake theologically. This is not to dismiss the metaphysical debate as meaningless or as totally irrelevant. That debate can continue with gusto for those who are interested; there is plenty of traditional material in ancient and contemporary philosophy to keep it alive. Too much theological reflection has, however, taken this course to be satisfactory. Hence the stale debates about immortality of the soul or resurrection of the body that were popular a generation ago. What matters initially is not metaphysical but theological in nature. What does God intend for the creatures he has created and redeemed? The crucial issues have to do with divine action.

Second, once we frame the issue aright it is immediately obvious that we can make little or no progress on this front without significant information on divine action and divine intentions. So how are we to go forward from here? Surely we are utterly dependent on special divine revelation at this point. We can only know what God has intended for us and thus what divine actions are involved if God reveals his intentions to us. I am so convinced of this basic epistemic principle that I am hard-pressed to understand why this observation is so readily ignored or set aside in disputes about life after death. The initial tendency is to reach for literature on near-death experiences, whether testimonial or formally scientific, and then settle for whatever the data warrant. There is a place for this material; and I shall come to it shortly. However, as a matter of epistemic principle these data cannot but be limited if not misleading, for they do not even begin to tackle the question about how to get access to the mind of God in creation and redemption.

What is at issue here can be stated succinctly and formally. Consider ordinary personal agents, that is, human agents. In broad terms they make themselves known by what they do, mostly through their bodily actions. We learn over time to read what our friends are doing by perceiving their behavior as set in a complex array of character, context, and convention. While not all of our actions are intentional actions (many are entirely accidental), intentional actions are identified by the intentions that govern them. Take the simple action of raising my hand in a room full of people. Did I raise my hand to answer a question or make a bid? The context and convention of the action will usually settle the issue. Where we are in doubt we generally ask the agent and the agent tells us. So raising a hand at an auction may not have been a bid if the agent tells us that she was actually waving at a friend who had just entered the room or was carrying out an exercise to relieve the pain in her left elbow. What people tell us is not infallible, but it is of enormous weight in sorting out how to identify the action and thus understand what is going on.

Now my own view is that God is best understood as a unique, tri-personal Trinitarian Agent. However, I do not need to defend this thesis here in order to point out that it is by analogy with human agents and how they reveal their intentions that we get access to what God is doing and intends in creation and redemption. God reveals his intentions and purposes by what God does; and identifying what God is doing depends on what God tells us. This applies even more saliently in the case because outside the incarnation God does not have a body. Hence in the case of God we are even more dependent on what God tells us in special revelation if we are to have access to the mind of God with respect to divine intentions and plans. I have argued at length elsewhere that this is precisely why the great tradition of thinking on this matter has insisted on the place of divine action and speaking as utterly central to any robust account of the mind of God in creation and redemption.

Applied to our question in hand, it is clear that the primary warrant for what we believe about life after death rests on what God has revealed to us in special revelation. The heart of the matter is best thought of in terms of what God has revealed and promised to us in the life, death, and resurrection of Jesus. In this instance, actions in deed and word, in resurrection and promise, are the bedrock phenomena. Put simply, we believe in the life to come because God has given us a foretaste of this proleptically in the resurrection of the Son and promised such life to all who repent and believe in his name. In and around this we can add the promise of our Lord to the thief on the cross and the assurances that shine through all over the scriptural record, as seen paradigmatically in the writings of Paul. We can sum it up this way: we believe in the life to come essentially because of faith, meaning by faith in this instance trust in God to carry out the promises he has given to us as now enshrined in scripture construed in part as the crucial medium of special revelation. This is precisely how it has been seen across the ages, and rightly so.

My own reading of this evidence took me exactly to the summary statement I articulated earlier. What God has promised us is an intermediate state on the dissolution of our bodies; eventually we will be raised to judgment and the resurrection of the body in a new heaven and a new earth. In this analysis I reject the claim commonly held in some evangelical circles that when we die we cease to exist until the resurrection of the dead in the last days. Equally, I set aside debates about the details of the intermediate state focused of late in the development of interesting proposals on purgatory within contemporary Protestantism. I am in fact thoroughly skeptical of any doctrine of purgatory; but that is an issue for another space and time. My primary concern is to stick to the big picture and argue the case for special revelation as the decisive warrant for Christian claims about life after death.

One other point before I move on. My appeal to special revelation readily welcomes the deployment of other theological considerations that may supplement the primary evidence involved. Thus I am particularly drawn to the general argument from God's overall actions in creation and redemption. It is surely odd to think that, given all that God has done in giving human agents a unique place in creation and in going to such lengths to redeem us, God has planned that our earthly life will be the end of us. Just as God cannot in his heart abandon earthly Israel but will preserve it for all time whatever their sin and whatever their opposition, so God will not abandon spiritual Israel to extinction in physical death. I would treat as less secure but certainly not as irrelevant metaphysical arguments about the nature of the soul; while there is no decisive proof, I suspect that souls are more like numbers than like atomic particles.

What then about arguments from near-death experiences and related phenomena? How does this fit into the argument I am making about relevant evidence for life after death? The evidence available is both anecdotal and scientific. Let me schematically present it before assessing its relevance and its worth.

Let me cite one anecdote from my own experience. Some years ago a student alerted me to the arrival of an Eastern Orthodox priest who was serving a small United Methodist church in East Texas. His name was Father George Rodonaia. I visited him in the parsonage and met his wife and children. His wife had a real problem with snakes in the garage. He found the habit of churchgoers leaving church early to watch the Dallas Cowboys on television astonishing. Over time I got to know him extremely well; indeed we became almost instant friends.

Originally from Georgia in the Soviet Union, he had been something of a rebel as a teenager and was naturally marked out as a troublemaker by the authorities. In time he became a dissident. After a brief run-in with the KGB at the age of fourteen, he resolved to fight the system by developing his intellect. By the time he was twenty-two he had a PhD, but his work as a research scientist in the early 1970s (cutting-edge study of neurotransmitters such as oxytocin and adenosine triphosphate) in conjunction with his political views turned out to be a dangerous combination. So in 1976 he decided to get out. He somehow got in touch with folk related to Senator John Tower of Texas and managed to obtain a US visa. The plan was that his wife would leave their apartment first and wait for him at the airport. But while he stood on the sidewalk waiting for his cab, a passing car jumped the curb and ran over him. He was taken to the hospital where, after several attempts at resuscitation, he was pronounced dead. The "accident" had been a hit-and-run affair; he was utterly convinced that the KGB were behind it.

George (or Yuri, as he was then known) was put on a refrigerated slab in the morgue and left in total darkness for three days. On a Monday morning he was taken out and the pathologists began the autopsy, making an incision in his abdomen. At that point his eyes opened and they realized he was alive. (He reported that thereafter they would not carry out autopsies.) Shortly afterward, they rang the Orthodox cathedral in Tbilisi and announced that they had "one of theirs" in the hospital; he had come back from the dead so they needed to take care of him. Recovery, of course, was not instantaneous; both his lungs had collapsed, and George reported being on a respirator for ninety days. After his discharge, though, he began to frequent the cathedral, and after further academic studies he became in turn a deacon and a priest. By all accounts he was a popular preacher and priest, so much so that there were crowds at early-morning services. Indeed he became so popular that the civil authorities put pressure on the church to move him to a remote place where he would not be so influential. There he became as popular as ever. So the pressure on him became so great that he got in touch with friends in Texas in order to find a way to leave Georgia. Eventually he made it out with his family and ended up in East Texas, working in the Texas Conference of the United Methodist Church.

He recounted in detail his experience in the morgue during that period when he was pronounced dead. Aside from his account of experiencing an amazing white light and incredible peace (standard features of such stories), I specifically recall two elements. First, he could see from above what the pathologists were doing when they began the autopsy. Second, he recalled vividly his awareness of a favorite aunt thinking about him and mourning his death. When he told her of this later and described exactly what she had been thinking, she was so afraid of what happened that she would not speak to him again. Later written accounts of his experience tell of his communicating—wordlessly—with a young child and diagnosing a greenstick fracture that had been missed by the attending physicians and was causing continual pain. When he later told the child's parents what was wrong, the diagnosis was confirmed as accurate. The outcome of this experience was what might be expected: he was totally unafraid of death and was totally convinced of the reality of the divine world.[1]

For my part I have no reason to disbelieve what Father George told me. His testimony was clear, sincere, humorous, and utterly believable. Without good reason to believe otherwise, I would find it very difficult not to take it with the utmost seriousness. We all know that there is a wealth of such anecdotal material on the worldwide web and in truckloads of books. Indeed Father George's case is identified as one of the most interesting within the circle of people who collect this material. For me this is more than a casual anecdote picked up off the web; I knew the person involved and had many conversations with him.

Things become even more interesting when we turn from anecdotal material to serious scientific investigation. The most rigorous work I know of has been provided by Pim van Lommel, a cardiologist in Holland. Van Lommel first presented his work in the medical journal, *The Lancet*, and went on to provide a full-scale treatment of the relevant issues in his book, *Consciousness beyond Life: The Science of Near-Death Experience*. His aim has been to provide a rigorous, objective study of the data related to near-death experience. What makes his work especially noteworthy, aside from the intellectual standards involved, is the fact that it made a prospective rather than a retrospective study of the subjects involved. The former allows for comprehensive observation of all medical and other data in the wake of a near-death experience. He is also interested in the practical implications of his work for healthcare.

In an overview of the data, van Lommel charts twelve elements that he detected in near-death experiences, providing striking examples to illustrate what is at stake. The following is the laundry list of elements: ineffability, a feeling of peace and quiet, the awareness of being dead, an out-of-body experience, a dark space, the perception of an unearthly environment, meeting and communicating with deceased persons, the perception of a brilliant light or a being of light, the panoramic life review, the preview or flash-forward, the perception of a border, and the conscious return to the body. Van Lommel goes on to chart the significant life changes that result from these experiences, consequences that are analogous to significant perceptual experience that are conventional. These include such changes as compassion for others, no fear of death, greater spirituality, and the like. He charts earlier accounts of near-death experiences across cultures and instances of near-death experiences in childhood. He also provides a systematic rebuttal of efforts to undermine the veridicality of the perception involved such as chemical and electrical activity in the brain, and various psychological explanations such as fear of death, deceit, and hallucination. He pursues the issues into the domain of quantum physics, following a lead developed by the renowned physicist Henry Stapp; and he enters the philosophical arena in his articulation of a vision of endless and nonlocal consciousness. One of the fundamental implications of his work is that it challenges at its very core "a purely materialistic scientific paradigm."[2]

Permit one example to give a sense of the shock involved

in coming to terms with the work of van Lommel. Here is the case as reported.

> During my NDE following a cardiac arrest, I saw both my dead grandmother and a man who looked at me lovingly but whom I didn't know. Over ten years later my mother confided on her death-bed that I'd been born from an extramarital affair; my biological father was a Jewish man who'd been deported and killed in World War II. My mother showed me a photograph. The unfamiliar man I'd seen more than ten years earlier during my NDE turned out to be my biological father.[3]

What is important about a case like this is the unique information conveyed in this particular near-death experience. Of course, one can always challenge the testimony; or one can disparage its accuracy by appeal to some kind of metaphysical principle that rules out the possibility of such information. However, one can at least insist that from a rational point of view the simpler explanation is that what the subject reported is true and then seek to rework one's standards of testimony and one's metaphysical commitments to fit with this alternative account.

We are now in a position to take up the question that lies before us. How far, if at all, does this network of anecdotal and scientific evidence support Christian claims about life after death as enunciated earlier? Note here that I am not going to take up the issue of what other elements, say, in theological anthropology, this material may support. It is obvious that these data call into question a purely materialistic conception of human agency and go some way to underwriting claims about the existence of the soul. The data also confirm

Christian claims that focus on God as described in terms of light and love, of experiences of the divine as ineffable, and of human beings as inescapably moral agents aware of moral good and evil. Our focus is more limited. Once we frame the matter carefully in terms of personal eschatology, then the conclusion is obvious: the data provide only limited support for Christian claims about personal eschatology. They provide warrant for the claim that we are right in believing that death is not the end of human existence; that we enter a whole new world on the dissolution of our bodies. However, note that they say nothing about divine action in relation to the afterlife. Moreover, they tell us absolutely nothing about the nature of the intermediate state beyond its initial stages, and they are totally silent on the issue of the resurrection of the body in a new and transformed creation.

Even so, I do not think we should underestimate the apologetic significance of this material. Much of our thinking in the West is saturated with the assumption that we can and should privilege empirical considerations from perception and science in sorting out what is true or false about the world. More broadly there is a kind of default reliance on materialism and scientism that is championed, for example, by the network of new atheists who have hammered this home with relentless enthusiasm. It is no accident that this evidence from near-death experiences is either ignored or dismissed by those committed to these assumptions. Perhaps the most famous example is furnished by the case of Sir Alfred Ayer, the great champion of logical positivism in his day. Initially his near-death experience really rattled him; in time he found ways to discount its epistemic significance. Here is how one scholar captures the situation.

[In June 1988] Ayer experienced a near-death experience (NDE). Three months after the experience he wrote an article about it, "What I saw when I was Dead." Ayer's account—very colourful—recounts crossing the river and concluded that the episode had done nothing to weaken his belief that God does not exist. Yet that was not the end of the story. Years later, Ayer's attending physician, Dr. Jeremy George, told William Cash that he had spoken with Ayer the same day Ayer had the NDE and asked him what it was like as a philosopher to experience an NDE. Ayer answered, "I saw a Divine Being. I'm afraid I'm going to have to revise all my various books and opinions." When Dr. George read Ayer's account he was surprised that Ayer had left out any mention of that. George's impression was that Ayer ". . . had come face to face with God, or his maker, or what one might say was God." Ayer's step son-in-law, Peter Foges, wrote that he had no reason to doubt Dr. George's testimony and that Ayer, when he wrote the two articles about his experience, was determined to preserve his public reputation, "of which he was almost childishly proud," of being one of Britain's most famous atheists. The first article Ayer wrote was published in *The London Telegraph*, and the second one was an addendum in *The Spectator*. Publicly, Ayer maintained that he was not affected by the religious implications of the NDE, but privately it was another matter. Those who knew him best noted how Freddie (Ayer) had changed. After the NDE his wife maintained that he was much nicer. "He was not nearly so boastful. He took an interest in other people." Ayer also spent a great deal of time during the last year of his life in conversation with the renowned Jesuit philosopher, Father Frederick Copleston.[4]

Even when, unlike Ayer, we are prepared to take the data from near-death experiences on board, it is patently obvious that they can be integrated into a significant number of competing interpretations that are internally inconsistent and that call into question a Christian vision of life after death. Van Lommel's foray into the metaphysics of quantum physics and his speculations about an endless and nonlocal consciousness represent this kind of case. Far from being irrational, they present a respected researcher trying to figure out the wider significance of his studies. What they suggest is that all sides involved, theistic and nontheistic, should take responsibility for spelling out the wider narratives and worldviews that they inevitably inhabit and within which they can then place the data of near-death experiences. Christian theologians have taken to heart the challenge of articulating and defending their wider narratives across the centuries, whereas more recent atheists have been content to engage for the most part in negative polemics and angry denunciation. They have failed to spell out what precise vision of life and of the world they are proposing, to specify the relevant evidence in its favor, to reflect epistemologically on what counts as relevant evidence, and to think through carefully about relevant objections that have to be addressed. As I have argued elsewhere, I am tempted to say that they have been intellectually cheating. I would not for a moment say this about the work of van Lommel. His work is a model of intellectual virtue and care. He is genuinely seeking to integrate his findings into a more comprehensive vision of consciousness and the world as a whole.

This work of integration is exactly what the theologian should also do without pretension and without overdetermining the apologetic and epistemic significance of the evidence. The Christian vision of life after death hinges on divine revelation. As such it dovetails with much of the evidence available from near-death experiences. We might say that the evidence from near-death experiences provides partial empirical confirmation of Christian claims about life after death and that it indirectly challenges some longstanding prejudices against taking the claims of divine revelation seriously. In the current climate of opinion these considerations are to be welcomed. However, they do not alter the fundamental warrants for what we rightly believe about life after death. These warrants are secured in the promises of God enacted in the resurrection of Jesus Christ and reiterated in their scriptural restatement in the New Testament, most clearly in Paul. In the very nature of the case the evidence from near-death experiences is strictly limited. The Christian claim is much deeper in that it involves claims about divine action (it is God who has promised life beyond the grave and who will ensure its reality). The Christian claim is also much more comprehensive, as it takes into its purview final judgment and the resurrection of the body.

One other feature of the Christian claim deserves mention in closing. In an astonishing assertion Paul, working off a text in Isaiah 64, insists that " 'what no eye has seen nor ear heard nor the human heart conceived, what God has prepared for those who love him,' these things God has revealed to us through the Spirit" (1 Cor. 2:9–10). This comment surely puts a limit to the possibility of any kind of empirical evidence taking us very far in understanding the life to come. That life will be so glorious that every effort to understand it in terms of our current human categories will fail. We get a hint of this in the remarks about ineffability that show up in reports of near-death experience. However, the Pauline claim is much more radical; it calls for drastic epistemic caution that will be overcome only in the actual experience of the life to come as made known to us beyond the grave. Even so, Paul insists we can have some sense of what is at stake in the reception of the mind of Christ here and now, a mind not available to those who do not have the Spirit. We can surely take this in part to mean that the believer has some sense of what is at stake and with that, a real assurance of the good things in store in the life to come. As we shall see in the next chapter, reference to assurance opens up another interesting tension that crops up in consideration of life after death—the tension between assurance and hope.

CHAPTER 3

Assurance and Hope

In the last chapter I ended with a strong endorsement of the claim that Christians can and should have assurance of the life to come. To put the matter more forthrightly, they can have certainty about the extraordinary future promised by God in the gospel and its enactment in the death and resurrection of Christ. If we need an example, the apostle Paul comes immediately to mind.

> For me, living is Christ and dying is gain. If I am to live in the flesh, that means fruitful labor for me; and I do not know which I prefer. I am hard pressed between the two: my desire is to depart and to be with Christ, for that is far better; but to remain in the flesh is more necessary for you. (Phil. 1:21–24)

> For we know that if the earthly tent we live in is destroyed, we have a building from God, a house not made with hands, eternal in the heavens. For in this tent we groan, longing to be clothed with our heavenly dwelling—if in-

deed, when we have taken it off we will not be found na-
ked. For while we are still in this tent, we groan under our
burden, because we wish not to be unclothed but to be
further clothed, so that what is mortal may be swallowed
up by life. He who has prepared us for this very thing is
God, who has given us the Spirit as a guarantee. (2 Cor.
5:1–5)

Equally, Paul fits the bill of a believer who can naturally
speak in terms of hope when it comes to life after death. In his
vigorous defense of the resurrection of Jesus he explicitly ex-
presses his convictions about the life to come in terms of hope.

If Christ has not been raised, your faith is futile and you
are still in your sins. Then these also who have died in
Christ have perished. If for this life only we have hoped
in Christ, we are of all people most to be pitied. (1 Cor.
15:17–19)

A wonderful passage from Colossians fits neatly with
this way of thinking of the future.

In our prayers for you we always thank God, the Father of
our Lord Jesus Christ, for we have heard of your faith in
Christ Jesus and of the love that you have for all the saints,
because of the hope laid up for you in heaven. You have
heard of this hope before in the word of truth, the gospel
that has come to you. (Col. 1:3–6)

We witness in this instance the familiar trinity of faith,
hope, and love as found in the famous passage of 1 Corinthi-
ans 13. It is worth noting the way in which Paul pictures our

epistemic situation with respect to the future in that famous text.

> Love never ends. But as for prophecies, they will come to an end; as for tongues, they will cease; as for knowledge, it will come to an end. For we know only in part, and we prophesy only in part; but when the complete comes, the partial will come to an end. When I was a child, I spoke like a child, I thought like a child, I reasoned like a child; when I became an adult, I put an end to childish ways. For now we see in a mirror, dimly, but then we will see face to face. Now I know only in part; then I will know fully, even as I have been fully known. And now faith, hope, and love abide, these three; and the greatest of these is love. (1 Cor. 13:8–13)

Most Christians will read the Pauline material on assurance and hope without batting an eyelid. However, there is an interesting dilemma that is worth pondering. To put the issue in its simplest form: we do not normally hope for things that we believe are assured. We can restate the dilemma more formally in this fashion.[1] On the one hand, it is natural to say that those who believe in life after death hope that there will be a life after death. They ardently desire that there be the kind of eternal life promised in the gospel; yet, if they hope this to be the case, they are not certain that this is the case. Hope rules out certainty; if we hope for a sunny afternoon, it is necessarily the case that we are not certain that there will be a sunny afternoon. On the other hand, it would appear that those who believe in a life after death may also naturally say that they are certain that there is life after death. They have assurance that there is a life after death. So there is a serious dilemma for the believer. It would appear that the believer is committed to not being certain and to being certain at one and the same time. If one is certain that there is a life after death, then speaking of hope makes no sense in this instance. If one hopes for a life to come, then this rules out assurance about a life to come.

Permit a short technical interlude to make the issue as clear as possible. We need at this point a more carefully crafted account of the logic of hope and the logic of assurance if we are to see what is at issue and resolve the puzzle before us. In what follows, let p stand for any proposition you like.

The conventional analysis of hope insists that hope is governed by two and only two essential conditions.[2] For A to hope that p entails, first, that A desires that p, and, second, A does not know that p. Here p is a proposition-variable and as a potential state of affairs constitutes the intensional object of hoping. So if I hope that tomorrow will be a sunny day for Murphy's wedding, I desire or wish that tomorrow will be a sunny day, and I do not know that tomorrow will be a sunny day. Generally these two conditions, desiring p and not knowing p, are taken to be jointly necessary and sufficient for hope.

As a disposition, hoping for p differs from merely believing that p. The crucial difference is that I can believe that p without hoping that p. So I may believe that tomorrow will be a sunny day without wishing that tomorrow be a sunny day. Of course, in hoping that p, various beliefs may be presupposed. So hoping for a sunny day for Murphy's wedding presupposes that I believe that Murphy exists, that his wedding is set for tomorrow, that there will be a tomorrow, that there will be weather of one sort or another, and so on. Equally, as a disposition, hoping that p is different from having an emotion, even though hope may be accompanied by various emotions. So my hoping that tomorrow will be a sunny day for Murphy's wedding may be accompanied by immediate sensations of warmth and happiness for Murphy, but this is not a necessary condition of my hoping that tomorrow will be a sunny day for Murphy's wedding. Having an emotion, say, being angry at Murphy for getting married tomorrow, is an occurrent process; whereas a disposition like hoping is a state of affairs that holds even when I am asleep or when I daydream about a break from work and have completely forgotten about Murphy's wedding on the next day.

As a disposition, hope has four contraries: fear, resignation, despair, and desperation. Contraries here are to be distinguished from contradictions. In the case of a contradiction, not-p is incompatible with p, and given the law of excluded middle, it is not the case that both p and not-p. In the case of contraries, a third alternative is possible. So I may neither hope nor fear p because I am totally indifferent to p. We can state the contraries straightforwardly in this manner. A hopes that p means that A desires that p and does not know that p. A fears that p means that p desires not-p but thinks that p is going to happen. A is resigned that p means that A wishes not-p but thinks that p is certain. A despairs that p means that A wishes that p but thinks that p is contracertain and gives up on taking any action. A is desperate with respect to p means that A wishes that p and A thinks that p is contracertain but is unlikely to do anything that might bring about p. This last observation indicates an interesting connection between hope and action, namely, that if A hopes that p, A, where possible and appropriate, will take action to bring about p.

My remarks so far have focused on the generic logical grammar of hope. Thus I have articulated a conventional account of hope as being governed by two conditions (desiring p and not knowing that p), which are jointly necessary and sufficient for hoping for this or that state of affairs. I have also indicated that hoping that p has an intensional object; that hoping implies taking relevant action to bring about p; and that hoping that p, as a disposition, is not to be confused with believing that p, having an emotion about p, or imagining that p.

Now let's take a look at the idea of assurance. A concept in the neighborhood of assurance that has received a lot of attention is the concept of certainty. So let's begin there. Let's treat assurance and certainty as synonymous. Consider the following crucial distinctions related to the kinds of certainty we readily identify.

A first kind of certainty is that of strong epistemic certainty. In this instance the belief that p enjoys the highest epistemic status possible. In this case we are thinking of our beliefs on a scale where we start at the bottom and believe that p is absolutely false and end at the top where it is absolutely true. We then index certainty to the measure of truth attributed to p, ranking certainty with p being true absolutely.

A second kind of certainty is that of moral certainty. In this instance we are dealing with a weaker epistemic conception of certainty, that is, one where the proposition enjoys a lesser degree of epistemic warrant than that available in the case of strong epistemic certainty. Descartes captured the notion in this way. "Moral certainty is certainty which is sufficient to regulate our behavior, or which measures up to the certainty we have on matters relating to the conduct of life which we never normally doubt, though we know that it is possible, absolutely speaking, that they may be false."[3] One way to put this is to say that the belief *p* is rational to a very high degree.

A third kind of certainty is psychological certainty. A person is psychologically certain of *p* when he or she is supremely convinced of the truth of *p*. This is not to be confused with incorrigibility. A proposition *p* is incorrigible when it is not possible for the person to abandon *p*. Being certain in the psychological sense, however, is subject to revision in the light of new evidence; being incorrigible is not so.

What kind of certainty should we attribute to Paul and to the mature believer in a life after death? I think a case can be made for attributing all three kinds of certainty to the believer. Contrary to popular and repeatedly asserted philosophical judgment, I think it is entirely possible for the believer to hold the first kind of epistemic certainty. How so? It is so precisely because belief in life after death is a matter of divine revelation. Divine revelation is nothing less than God's own knowledge made available to us. Consider an analogy. I know, say, that there will be a final exam in the course because I set it. Students in turn will know because I tell them. God knows what the future holds for the creatures made in his image because God has designed and planned a glorious future for them in the life to come. We know what God has planned because God has revealed it to us in the gospel. We have God's own Word for it, a Word we can utterly rely on. This is the conception of revelation one finds, for example, in Aquinas. He thought that this was the highest kind of knowledge, and I think Aquinas was right about this and that moderns and postmoderns are wrong. However, because there are deep complications and considerable skepticism related to this claim, I will set it aside here.[4]

We can surely allow for the possibility of the believer having moral certainty. This is a notch below strong epistemic certainty. In this case the believer has the kind of certainty about life after death that she normally has with an assortment of other beliefs that are sufficiently warranted to regulate her belief and action. We might include such beliefs as that Barack Obama was president of the USA in April 2016, that I currently own two English cocker spaniels called Sophie and Murphy, that California suffered severe water problems in the summer of 2015, and the like. Absolutely speaking, all of these propositions could be false. Until I know that this is the case, I will continue to hold them with moral certainty. So we can think of a mature believer who is morally convinced that there is life after death but who would readily concede that this claim could be false, say, because it turns out to be incoherent; or because the divine revelation on which it is based turns out to be spurious. It would not be difficult to find lots of recent examples of such moral certainty in the literature of persecution against Christians.

As for psychological certainty, the case for this possibility being an option for the believer is self-evident. It is surely possible for the believer to be supremely convinced that there is life after death. Many in the past have been supremely convinced that this is indeed the case and were prepared to give up their lives in martyrdom because of this conviction.

There are some very easy ways of solving the dilemma that we set aside without too much difficulty. First, we simply keep the references to hope and jettison the expressions of assurance or certainty. There are several reasons why we might do so. First, a lot of people, including serious Christian believers, instinctively gravitate to this kind of stance. They would naturally say that they hope there is a life to come of the kind proclaimed in the gospel, but they simply cannot bring themselves to believe for sure that this is the case. Thus they desire and wish it to be the case, but they are very clear that they are not sure this is the case. They are at home in the language of hope; they are ill at ease in the language of assurance. They are content to wait and see. Second, they may go a step further and insist that it is presumptuous to speak of being certain about there being a life after death. Typically, they will say that no one has come back from the other side; we simply do not have good enough evidence to say objectively that there is actually a life after death. So it is a mistake to be overconfident and claim too much, given what we already know, namely that when people die, they stay dead and do not come back to tell us if there is a life after death. So we can resolve our dilemma by dropping all talk of assurance when it comes to life beyond the grave.

For obvious reasons I do not find this line of reasoning at all persuasive. For one thing, someone *has* come back from the dead, even Jesus of Nazareth, and as Son of God, he has promised us eternal life in a life to come. I need not rehearse here the arguments given in the previous chapter that provide stable warrant for being assured that there is a life to come. There is adequate evidence in special revelation, partially supplemented by compelling empirical considerations. Thus I see reticence on the part of Christians to claim assurance as regards the life to come as driven by pressures from a skeptical and increasingly unbelieving culture and by a radical intellectual failure of nerve when it comes to the truth of the gospel. To be sure, I have heartfelt and keen sympathy with this kind of reticence. Moreover, there is an entirely sincere conception of faith that limits itself to hoping that the gospel is true and living accordingly. Furthermore, our sense of assurance may start out as a faltering faith and over time grow into something stronger and stronger. Paul stands out as an instance where there is deep and lasting assurance almost from the very beginning, but it is not essential that all believers be modeled on this example. What matters here is that the move to solve our dilemma by dropping assurance comes at much too high a price intellectually and spiritually.

Just imagine a world without the wonderful certainties of Paul and of the many great saints who exhibit this kind of certainty. Consider in this regard an astonishing passage from St. Symeon the New Theologian who not only notes the practices essential to growth in grace but brings that journey to a foretaste of the glory that is to be in heaven.

> I therefore entreat you, my fathers and brethren and children, let us endeavor to attain to purity of heart, which comes from paying heed to our ways and from constant confession of the secret thoughts of the soul. For if we, moved by a penitent heart, constantly and daily confess these, it produces in us repentance for what we have done and even thought. Repentance gives rise to the tear from the depths of the soul; the tear cleanses the heart and wipes away great sins. When these have been blotted out through tears the soul finds itself in the comfort of the Spirit of God and is watered by tears of sweetest compunction. By these it is spiritually fructified day by day so that it produces the fruits of the Spirit (Gal. 5: 22f) and in due time yields them like an abundant harvest of grain as an unfailing supply of food for the incorruptible and

eternal life of the soul. When the soul by a good zeal has reached this state it is identified with God and becomes the house and the abode of the divine Trinity. It sees its own Maker and God clearly, and as it converses with him day by day it departs from the body and the world and from this air and ascends into the heaven of heavens. Borne aloft by the virtues and by the wings of God's love it rests from its labors altogether with all the righteous and is found in the infinite and divine Light, where the hosts of Christ's apostles, of the martyrs, of the blessed ones and all the powers on high sing in chorus together.[5]

Surely our vision of the faith would be radically impoverished if we were to dismiss all this as pious fantasy or presumption. This is the ultimate *reductio ad absurdum* of the move to solve our dilemma by sticking with hope and abandoning assurance.

We could, of course, abandon hope and stick with assurance. I will not pursue this in any detail simply because, compared to abandoning assurance and sticking with hope, this is just not a serious option intuitively for most believers. Given the reticence about assurance and the inescapable place of hope in the Christian faith, if there is a conflict between retaining hope over against assurance, hope will win every time.

A less radical way out would be to resort to paradox. On this analysis we simply have to live with the fact that the dilemma cannot and should not be resolved. Like so much else in the Christian faith, we are faced with a paradox, that is, apparently contradictory commitments, or more radically with mystery, that is, with a dilemma that unlike a puzzle will never be resolved. Either way, we have simply reached the end of our intellectual capacities and we should rest there in faith. If hope and assurance can go together for Paul, then so be it; let the nit-picking of the minute philosophers and theologians be set aside; let's concentrate on developing both assurance and hope as spiritual virtues and note that life, especially our spiritual life, is larger than logic.

But surely a mature faith calls for the search for understanding; so we should take this way out only if there is no other way forward. Perhaps we have been too quick to rest with a conventional vision, say, of hope as it relates to assurance. And if we take a second look, maybe there are considerations in the neighborhood of Christian vision of life after death that might relieve us of the intellectual tension and thereby deepen our understanding.

Consider the following parable of the Phone Call at Midnight. Traveling alone in South Texas, your friend Seamus is kidnapped by a vicious drug gang known locally as the Bloodthirsty Bandits. The gang believes that Seamus comes from a rich family and their intention is to hold him until his family fork out a ransom of five million dollars. They give his family seven days to pay up; if they do not pay up, his family will find the mutilated body of their beloved on a backstreet of Corpus Christi. Seamus is informed of the ransom request and very naturally fears for his life, for he knows his family does not have this kind of money. For the most part Seamus is left alone, holed up in a makeshift hut down a deserted road that leads to nowhere. Surprisingly he has managed to hide his cell phone in his left boot, having carefully switched it to vibration mode. On the second day of his confinement he receives a phone call at midnight from a woman who claims to represent the local police department. She also identifies herself as a friend from the past, a fact that explains why her voice is so familiar. She tells him that she knows where he is located, that they are working on a rescue plan, and that he should look for confirmation of her promise of help by the sound if not sight of a helicopter near enough to be recognized but not close enough to sound the alarm among his captors. Much to his surprise the helicopter shows up as promised. A second phone call promises that the proposed rescue will take place at midnight on the sixth day of his confinement. His job is to lie low, cooperate with his captors, and wait for his deliverers to show up. He follows these instructions and is rescued at midnight on the sixth day as promised.

How should we describe Seamus's state of mind in the period before his rescue? Surely the natural disposition is precisely one of both assurance and hope. He has been given a promise that he will be rescued in the near future. But he is initially skeptical of the call, half-believing that it is a ruse by his captors to disorient him and prevent him from taking steps to escape. Even so, he is intuitively convinced that the promise is genuine; and this is confirmed by the sound and sight of the helicopter each day. Thus he has a genuine assurance that he will be rescued. Yet we can also describe his mental state as one of hope. He certainly desires the proposed outcome; yet he finds himself at times thinking that the whole story is too good to be true and that all sorts of contingencies could prevent it from happening. Perhaps his captors will move him to another location. Perhaps they will change their mind and simply kill him for the sheer hell of it. Perhaps his rescuers will botch the whole effort to rescue him.

This is a situation where it makes sense to speak of both hope and assurance. Because Seamus is relatively certain that the person who phoned him is genuine, his intellectual orientation is marked in this instance by assurance. Yet, because there is as yet no deliverance, his intellectual orientation is also marked by hope. There are two critical factors here that make this case stand out from conventional cases of hope. First, while Seamus is assured that his friend is reliable and above board, he does not understand what is going on in detail. His assurance is in the word of promise. Second, the future promised here is so extraordinary that he naturally would say that it is incredible. It is a case of a stupendous future that is beyond his ken in terms of how it will work. The knowledge of his friend is what grounds his assurance that the rescue will happen; the breathtaking content of the promised future is what makes it a subject of hope. It is a case where there is both moral certainty and hope directed to the same intensional object.

This is precisely how I think we should resolve the dilemma of hope and assurance as it relates to life after death. We have significant and adequate grounds for assurance that there will be a life after death as depicted in the promises of the gospel. Yet because the content of the promises involves a grace and glory beyond our comprehension, we readily treat it in terms of hope. Paul surely hints at this when he contrasts the knowledge we have now in Christ compared to the knowledge of what Christ will make available in the life to come. When he focuses on the first part, his mind is flooded with gratitude and assurance; when he focuses on the second, he has to resort to the language of hope. Now we see in a mirror dimly; then we shall see face to face. We have enough sight in the mirror to give us assurance; it is the gap between the sight here and the sight over there that creates the space for hope.

We do not therefore need to resort to paradox or mystery in resolving the relationship between hope and assurance. We are dealing here with a special case that breaks the neat and tidy categories that crop up when we limit our analysis to ordinary, run-of-the-mill cases. Such analysis gets the discussion up and running; it should not be our resting place. In dealing with life after death we can begin with our ordinary concepts of hope and assurance, but they are stretched by the sheer audacity of the claims that confront us in the gospel. In this case the stretching also dissolves the dilemma by bringing them together in a fitting harmony. We begin with ordinary wisdom and are transported to a divine wisdom that makes sense to those who have come to inhabit the rich canonical faith of the church so wonderfully embodied in so many of its great saints.

Indeed we can go all the way back to Abraham. Here is Paul's brilliant summary of his faith.

> Hoping against hope, he believed that he would become "the father of many nations," according to what was said, "So numerous shall your descendants be." He did not weaken in faith when he considered his own body, which was already as good as dead (for he was about a hundred years old), or when he considered the barrenness of Sarah's womb. No distrust made him waver concerning the promise of God, but he grew strong in his faith as he gave glory to God, being fully convinced that God was able to do what he had promised. (Rom. 4:18-21)

Think of Abraham's faith in this way. On the one hand, Abraham had come to enjoy intimate fellowship with God, sufficiently intimate to furnish an assurance that grew to the point where he was prepared to sacrifice his son Isaac, a crucial person relative to the promise of God to make him the father of many nations. On the other hand, such was the sheer audacity and impossibility of the content of the promise that it was also crucial to speak of it in terms of hope against hope. Hope and assurance, assurance and hope; both are natural for a faith that is vouchsafed by the great promises of the gospel and that contains elements that are an extraordinary and incomprehensible gift of God in the life to come.

One way to think of what I have done in this chapter is to turn the tables on those who insist that our lack of definitive and comprehensive knowledge of the afterlife is a liability for the Christian believer. As I noted earlier, Paul insists that what God has in store for those who love him is strictly speaking inconceivable as we continue our pilgrim way in this life. This is not to say we know nothing, for we know a foretaste of it here and now through life in the Spirit. We also know that the promises of God underwrite the inconceivable glory that is to come. We are given an assurance by God as to what is in store for us. Perhaps this is one reason why the tradition prefers to speak of assurance rather than certainty, even though there are obvious resonances in place. Our knowledge of life beyond the grave is genuine but strictly limited in that all we have is the big picture rather than the details. Even more so, it is strictly limited by the cognitive capacities, linguistic resources, and skills that we currently possess. Yet these limitations are not something to bemoan and lament. They are something to celebrate and ponder with care. They allow us to practice the virtue of hope even as we humbly anticipate the amazing future that God in his love and mercy has for us. Hence our semantic and epistemic limitations create the space for spiritual growth and development. They are a precious asset rather than a fatal liability.

Even so, we recognize that it helps in the cultivation of hope when we can envisage, however fitfully and inadequately, what is in store for us. Imagining what the future holds can be a spur to hope even though strictly speaking it is not essential to hope. Happily, the tradition recognizes this and copes with it by piling up the images to describe what lies ahead of us. It speaks of "palms, crowns, white robes, thrones, and splendor like the sun and stars."[6] We hear about pearly gates, streets paved with gold, and a mansion with many rooms, a day with no more night, a river of life, a heavenly city, and a Lamb at the center of the throne. Only a fool will want to take these *au pied de la lettre*; they are graphic and diverse precisely because they cannot be taken literally. We find this same use of imagery also showing up in attempts to describe the rich experiences of the Holy Spirit that are to be found in the tradition and that are a foretaste of the heaven to come.[7]

Let me finish with two examples that begin to open up a whole new topic for discussion that cannot be pursued here.

Consider this subtle passage from Teresa of Avila. Notice how Teresa draws on the analogy of two people in love in order to understand the dialectic between understanding her experience of God here and now and anticipating our experience of God in heaven.

It seems to me that the Lord in every way wants this soul [and by extension all believers] to have some knowledge of what goes on in heaven. I think that just as in heaven you understand without speaking (which I certainly never knew until the Lord in His Goodness desired that I should see and showed Himself to me in a rapture), so it is in this vision. For God and the soul understand each other only through the desire His Majesty has that it understand Him, without the use of any other means devised to manifest the love these two friends have for each other. It's like the experience of two persons here on earth who love each other deeply and understand each other well; even without the signs, just by a glance, it seems, they understand each other. This must be similar to what happens in the vision; without our knowing how, these two lovers gaze directly at each other, as the Bridegroom says to the Bride in the Song of Songs.[8]

The image of the bride shows up in a very different time and place, this time in the words of the great Baptist missionary to Burma, Adoniram Judson. Notice how he adds an additional image of transition from one state to another that informs his use of the image of the bride.

Lying here on my bed, when I could not talk, I have had such views of the loving condescension of Christ, and the glories of heaven, as I believe are seldom given to mortal man. It is not because I shrink from death that I wish to live, neither is it because the ties that bind me here, though some of them are very sweet, bear any comparison with the drawings I at times feel toward heaven; but a few years would not be missed from my eternity of bliss, and I can well afford to spare them, both for your sake and for the sake of the poor Burmans.

I am not tired of my work, neither am I tired of the world; yet when Christ calls me home, I shall go with the gladness of a boy bounding away from school. Perhaps I felt something like the young bride, when she contemplates resigning the pleasant associations of her childhood for yet a dearer home—though only a very little like her, for *there is no doubt resting on my future.*[9]

Understanding the beauty and wonder of the life to come is intrinsically important for faith. It is also the key to explaining the subtle combination of hope and assurance about the life to come that is the mark of robust believers.

CHAPTER 4

Another Look at the Suffering of Job

The good things that God has prepared for us in the life to come are strictly inconceivable in this life. We cannot capture the providence of God at work in future blessing other than by resort to a plethora of incompatible metaphors and symbols. These metaphors and symbols are reality-depicting; they are not mere metaphors and symbols. Indeed the reality far outstrips the language in terms of its abundance and brilliance. In the end we will, by grace and mercy, see for ourselves what God has in store for us. How and why all this has been planned and arranged constitutes a genuine mystery that is beyond our current capacities to understand. It is tempting to speculate that on the other side we will understand the details because of some radical alteration in our semantic and epistemic capacities. This surely is nothing but gossipy conjecture at this point. We have to work with the capacities and resources we currently possess; anything beyond this is strictly off limits for now. The wise course is to stick to the rough ground of our finite human capacities.

We face a similar challenge with respect to our understanding of providence in the case of suffering and grief in the face of death. There is an intriguing symmetry between the incomprehensibility of blessing and the incomprehensibility of suffering. I plan to show this in this chapter by a fresh reading of the book of Job. In working with Job we come back full circle to where we began, namely, to massive grief at the loss of a loved one. In Job's case it is multiplied by a factor of ten. In dealing with Job we also get a glimpse of the crucial place of experience of the divine as a counterweight to the incomprehensibility of suffering.

The book of Job is essentially a book about faith. James in the New Testament insists on Job as a call to patience. This fits with my reading of the book. However, there is much more to Job than a platitude about the significance of patience for faith. The book of Job also provides illumination of the proper motivation for faith, its intense internal conflicts, its ultimate survival, and its fundamental logic and character.

The book opens with a neat description of Job as a man of faith. He is blameless and upright; he rightly fears God, standing in awe of God and fearful of the consequences of disobeying God; he is morally active and energetic, setting his face against wrongdoing. We should also note that he is a man committed to scrupulous religious practice. After his children indulge in various banquets he sends for them to sanctify them. Perhaps uncertain of what they may have been up to, he makes a whole-offering before God for them. To top it all he is the greatest man in the East, a man abundantly prosperous in terms of worldly possessions and honor.

The drama of the book is generated by his prosperity.

What will happen to Job if God removes his prosperity? Will he remain blameless and upright, fearing God, and steadfastly setting his face against evil? Or will he turn and curse God, as his wife so poignantly advises? This raises the question of the deep motivation for his relationship with God. Is it initiated and sustained by material prosperity? If prosperity is replaced by adversity and suffering, what will happen to his spiritual and moral commitments? This question, introduced by the enigmatic figure of Satan, is the hinge of the book.

When we turn to the end of the book we find two factors, one more implicit and one more explicit, that are not mentioned at the beginning but that also provide illuminating information as we encounter Job at the beginning. If we take Job as a paradigm of traditional piety, it is clear that he is intellectually self-sufficient and relaxed. We might say that he is theologically smug. He has never pondered the challenge that suffering poses to his theology. As a creature he exhibits an implicit faith in his own ability to unravel the nature of divine providence. In addition, at the end of the book Job makes the startling admission not just that he was intellectually overconfident but that his faith was essentially a matter of hearsay and tradition rather than of ultimate encounter and firsthand experience. He had descriptive knowledge of God handed down across the generations; he did not have first-order acquaintance with God. This too is an important feature of the Job we meet at the beginning of the dialogical drama.

At the very end of the book, some of what we see at the beginning is still in place. He is a loyal priest who makes a burnt offering for his estranged friends who have rudely excoriated his protests with increasing gusto and nastiness. He is a man approved of God, despite his heart-rending protests and his boldness in insisting that God show up in court to answer the charges against him. He is abundantly prosperous again, the recipient of massive divine blessings. However, in addition he is intellectually chastened and humbled. He recognizes the severe limitations of his creaturely capacity to understand the workings of divine action in creation, in society, and in his own personal life. Perhaps most important of all, given its literary placement in the last words of Job, he has undergone a personal encounter with God that has moved beyond a third-person perspective on his faith to a first-person perspective.

Taken together, these two changes in Job make the book of Job a book of enormous significance in responding to the challenge of suffering. Job does not become a dualist where one parcels off the good in creation to God and the evil to Satan. Nor does he become the kind of modern skeptic who rests on the challenge of suffering as the crucial warrant to move initially to agnosticism and then to atheism. The designation of God as Yahweh, the God of Israel, late in the book makes it clear that he remains utterly committed to the theological heritage of Israel. The placing of the book itself in the canon of Israel's scriptures only strengthens this stance as seen in the final reception of the book as a whole. There is indeed revision of the received or conventional picture of the God of Israel as represented by the debate that makes up the core of the book. However, there is no rejection. There is significant first-order and second-order revision. The first-order revision involves a radical and aggressive rejection of the doctrine of providence represented by the tradition of the elders. The second-order revisions are epistemological, metaphysical, and spiritual. They are epistemological in that they relate to claims about knowledge of God and of divine action; they are metaphysical in that they relate to claims about divine causality in creation, society, and in our personal lives; they are spiritual in that they relate to the proper motivation for faith in the face of massive suffering.

As I have noted already, the book of Job is essentially a midrash on the nature of true faith. It is an amazing reflection on the transformation of Job brought about by the challenge of horrendous evil. At the outset Job would appear to have a faith that is predominantly external and conventional; at the end Job exhibits a faith that has not abandoned the faith of Israel but has been enriched by a person-relative encounter, face to face with God. On this front, his faith is marked by a retrieval of a vital element in the faith of Israel, that of intimate experience of God, which provides vital assurance in a pilgrimage challenged to its foundations by suffering. This is one way to chart the contrast. The second way draws attention to the intellectual transformation Job undergoes in the course of the book. At the outset he is theologically self-confident, if not overconfident, arrogant, and smug. At the very least he is intellectually asleep and insensible. By the end of the book he has been rudely awakened from his dogmatic slumbers and has become intellectually chastened and humbled. On this front, he is also tapping into the deep faith of Israel in its reserve about fathoming the mystery of the divine in this life.

The transition involved in this contrast between the beginning and end of the book of Job is extremely painful. It is in the details of this transition that we encounter the full force of suffering endured by Job. The initial torrent of pain is represented by the loss of his possessions at the hands of marauding neighbors, the appalling death of his ten beloved children due to a freak hurricane of nature, and the onset of a skin disease that reduces him to incessant pain, day and night. It is small wonder that his wife encourages him to curse God and die. There is surely a hint here of family conflict; think of the way in which sickness and death in a family can tear it apart, with no possibility of recovery and reunion.

It is small wonder that the first response to this series of calamities is a week of silence. Words simply fail him; he has gone into a black hole where nothing that is said or heard can make a difference. His semantic and cognitive capacities are overwhelmed with grief and agony. Happily, the friends who show up recognize this and join with Job in his silence.

The silence, however, can only last so long. We are creatures who think and speak, as Jews and Christians have done in their own ways from time immemorial. When Job breaks his silence, his language is the language of torment and agony. Job initially bursts into a fit of cursing. Yet he does not curse God; he curses in horrible detail the days of his conception and of his birth.

> "Let the day perish in which I was born,
> and the night that said,
> 'A man-child is conceived.'
> Let that day be darkness!
> May God above not seek it,
> or light shine on it.
> Let gloom and deep darkness claim it.
> Let clouds settle upon it;
> let the blackness of the day terrify it.
> That night—let thick darkness seize it!
> let it not rejoice among the days of the year;
> let it not come into the number of the months.

Yes, that it might be barren;
let no joyful cry be heard in it.
Let those curse it who curse the Sea,
those who are skilled to rouse up Leviathan.
Let the stars of its dawn be dark;
let it hope for light, but have none;
may it not see the eyelids of the morning—
because it did not shut the doors of my mother's womb,
and hide trouble from my eyes.
Why did I not die at birth,
come forth from the womb and expire?" (Job 3:3–11)

From cursing he turns to lament, lashing out with a barrage of questions as to why there were knees to receive him and breasts to suckle him, or why his longing for death is not answered.

At this point his friends intervene, gently at first, and then with a streak of mean intensity. Thus there begins a whole new cycle of suffering, this time at the hands of his friends. They move from friendly exhortation to nasty accusations as they seek to explain to Job what God is doing in and through the suffering he is enduring. We all surely know the agony of those disagreements that arise across the years when we find that friends we have loved and trusted intellectually take theological turns in the road that we find shocking and incredible. Perhaps in this case, because of our sympathy with Job, we fail to register the pain in the mind that his friends are facing, for it is Job who has departed from their cherished convictions, convictions without which their lives would fall apart. Even so, it is Job's suffering at the hands of his friends that gets our attention. When Job refuses even to answer the forceful arguments of his friends that are reintroduced by the young hotshot theologian at the end of these dialogues, we surely agree with his silence. Think of the newly tenured assistant professor, fresh out of graduate school, who cannot wait for the old guard to retire and get out of the way. We understand why Job simply ignores him.

Even though there is considerable subtlety at times in the dialogues, it is relatively easy to summarize the theological reasoning of Job's human interlocutors. There is a central claim that is repeated again and again. Its heart is a thesis about divine action; more precisely it is a thesis about the policy that governs all divine action in the world and in history. It states simply that God rewards the good person with prosperity; and God punishes the bad person with suffering and adversity. Life works essentially on a principle of moral reciprocity and retribution.

This is the wisdom that has been handed down across the generations and should not be challenged. To be sure, this policy is governed by an omniscience that we grasp only in a limited way. Our finite grasp of the infinite is limited; we are worms and maggots in our perspective when it comes to observing this crucial policy of divine providence. Moreover, it works more on the long-term rather than the short-term; those who hold to it will ultimately be vindicated by its historical verification. Most important of all, it is the rock-like foundation of our theological and spiritual world. If you reject it, you are not just mistaken; you are subject to self-deception. There is no room for entertaining criticism. If you challenge it you are full of arrogance and self-deceit. You are challenging God, a mere finite maggot taking on the Almighty. You should be personally vilified and socially shunned and shamed in order to bring you to your senses. The practical corollaries for Job are obvious. He should stop his cursing and lamenting; he should take another look at his life and identify his sins; then repent of his known and hidden sins; accept divine discipline; and return to God and prosper.

It is important to pause and take the measure of this whole way of thinking, for it is rampant in some Christian circles even today. You can make a fortune peddling it on television and in popular books. First, it is wonderfully simple; and generally we take simplicity as a mark of truth. Second, it is supported by significant empirical evidence. Third, it is spiritually cost-effective. It cuts through all the chatter and qualifications we hear about suffering, and gives us a plain principle that provides a hopeful way forwards. Fourth, it embodies the conventional wisdom handed down and embodies a receptive rather than skeptical attitude toward that tradition. Serious philosophers from Descartes to Burke to contemporary conservative thinkers have rightly insisted that tradition is to be taken seriously. This is not because of some postmodern platitude about all of us being enmeshed in personal and social contexts, but because tradition deserves our respect. It is more likely than not to embody the wisdom and experience of generations; in this respect the odd revolution here and there is the exception that proves the rule. Transferred to the theological experience of Israel, the lesson had long been advanced in the Deuteronomic history. Choose God and his ways and you will live; reject God and his ways and you will surely die. So Job should shut up and knuckle under. His experience is a mere drop in the ocean over against the wisdom of the ages.

Job's response to this conventional theology takes up nineteen of the twenty-seven chapters in this section. Again we have simplicity mixed with subtlety. As Job sees it, his critics are simply wrong. Their account of divine action involves a false reading of the universe and a false depiction of God. God does not operate by the policy that is ascribed to him. God acts uniformly in the lives of the good and the wicked; it is divine action all the way to the bottom. Job himself is the supreme counterexample. What he is enduring is not to be described as divine punishment because such a reading does not respect the distinction between the guilty and the innocent. Job is innocent; no matter what the intellectual or emotional pressure, he will not abandon this observation. His critics are not wise, as they think they are. Their theology is mistaken. He is right and they are wrong. He is not self-deceived; they are. He will not give up on his reasoning; he will carry it into the very courts where God will be summoned to hear his case face to face. In this setting God will vindicate him rather than reject his case. So Job does not even pause to reject explicitly their spiritual solution of self-examination, repentance, and return to God.

Note, however, the moments of subtlety that show up. Job wonders aloud whether there is any prosperity at all in this life; it looks as if life itself is simply short, nasty, and brutish all the way to the bottom. He agrees with the distinction between long-term and short-term analyses of the situation. He will not abandon the omnipresent action of God even when that includes suffering. He would rather say that he was being attacked head-on by God than say that God had gone on holiday and ceased to act in his life. He chides God for not initially answering his questions. All he wants is an office appointment at court with God because he still holds that God is the cause of his dreadful situation. He even hints at a solution. God's wisdom is inscrutable. There is no third party above God who can act as mediator and judge in this court case. We cannot in the end find wisdom; in fact the only wisdom available to us is to fear God and turn from evil. Whatever the qualifications of his protest, one thing remains secure: he is an innocent agent and this innocence undermines the standard theodicy that explains what happens in terms of a policy of reciprocity.

Even so, there is a stunning ambiguity buried in the debate about how to translate the Hebrew of Job 13:13–15. Here is the NRSV translation.

> Let me have silence, and I will speak,
> and let come on me what may.
> I will take my flesh in my teeth,
> and put my life in my hand.
> See, he will kill me; I have no hope;
> but I will defend my ways to his face.

A footnote to these verses provides the alternative reading to the final affirmation: "Though he kill me, yet I will trust in him." The latter reading is not just the more traditional reading; it may well have been the earliest reading in the manuscript tradition. Reading the book as a whole, we can see how editors wrestled theologically with both readings. In context the official translation given above is more fitting; yet theologically the second has its persuasive power when we come to the end of the book.

It is toward the end of the book that God eventually takes center stage. The attentive reader surely notes the suspense in play. After all the emotional and intellectual interchange of the human agents involved in the story, what will God do by way of response? Will God even show up? If God does show up, what will God say? Will he endorse

Job's critics and call for repentance? Or will he vindicate Job against his critics?

Across four chapters we are given a tour of creation where Job is called upon by God to explain what is going on. It moves by turns through the cosmos, through the meteorological phenomena of the weather, and through the wonders of the animal kingdom, with a brief interlude on the challenge of handling the wicked. The crucial question put to Job comes right at the start: "Where were you when I laid the foundations of the earth? Tell me, if you have understanding" (Job 38:4). Job in response simply capitulates. His last words are that he repents in dust and ashes.

It can readily appear to the skeptical reader that Job talks big when teacher is absent and then cowers in fear when teacher enters the room and confronts him with the gap between them. He will talk loud and long about the horrors of Stalinism behind Stalin's back, but cower in fear when the Big Man enters the room and begins his speech. However, this represents an adolescent and cynical reading of the text as a whole. I take the reference to dust and ashes to be a graphic expression set in spiritual terms of Job's heartfelt confession of human finitude and limitation. This is in keeping with the full-scale explicit confession of ignorance that comes earlier: "I have uttered what I did not understand, and things too wonderful for me, which I do not know." Yet this is not a confession of out-and-out agnosticism. Job acknowledges that God operates by means of divine purpose. Put technically, we might say that he insists that God is an omnipotent intentional agent. In his actions there is both power and design at work. However, God's ways are beyond our understanding.

The other element in Job's response is equally important. Where before Job had relied on God as a matter of the hearing of the ear, now he has come to see God face to face. He has met the God of Israel for himself, so the options of agnosticism and atheism (however culturally anachronistic it may be to apply them here) are nonstarters. Job returns to his job as a priest and intercessor, accepting the burnt offering of his erstwhile critics. Approved by God for saying what is right, his fortunes are lavishly restored. Included within this is an outpouring of sympathy and compassion from his family and friends.

Reviewing the book as a whole, we can readily see the intricate depths to which the writer has taken us in this treatment of suffering, including the suffering associated with acute grief. We see how intense suffering readily leads to silence and psychological meltdown. We move from initial horror and agony to silence; then on through cursing and lament to radical questioning and debate; and we end up with radical intellectual and spiritual reorientation. In this complex process it is crucial that we have folk around us who share in our silence even as they cannot share in our misery. As we move beyond this we also need friends and critics to push us through our cursing and lamentation to tackle the agonizing questions about life and about God that are inescapable. We may not like our critics and readily resort, as Job does, to polemic and excoriation. This is the way things are intellectually; academic life is riddled with nastiness and intellectual vice. When we meet this, we are not served by retreating into pious platitude and nonsense but by forthright confrontation and argument that takes the issues all the way to the bottom. Reorientation means pain as much as it ends in relief, as graduate students often find to their surprise.

This reorientation does not undercut the relation be-

tween commitment and blessing, but the experience of
suffering decimates any simplistic causal claim about the
relation between commitment and blessing and between
rebellion and disaster. It qualifies a very natural inference
that arises again and again from within divine revelation and
the action of providence as seen in the promises of blessing
given to us by grace in faith. We constantly run the risk of
running ahead of ourselves, grounded in the best of insights,
only to find that the whole edifice is in danger of crashing
down around our ears.

I speak here of qualification. It is important to take the
measure of that qualification. Initially it undercuts efforts to
explain exactly why God causes or permits the calamitous
events that often hit us like a bolt from the blue. By explanation I mean a teleological action in which we explain why
an agent does something in order to achieve certain intentions and purposes. So God brings about suffering to teach
us a lesson we could not otherwise learn for ourselves; the
suffering exists in order to achieve a higher good. In the case
of Job's critics the explanation for Job's suffering was that he
was an unrepentant sinner. So God sent suffering to punish
him and to further a greater good, that is, to bring him to
repentance and back to a life of prosperity. It is this whole
way of thinking that is called into question. We cannot give
such an explanation, surely in part, from lack of all the relevant information. This is part of the lesson of the long divine
speech that begins with the query as to where we were when
God laid the foundations of the earth. However, it surely
goes further, in that Job also insists that there is no neutral
judge who can resolve the disputes that arise when we question God's ways of working across creation, society, and our
own personal lives. This dovetails with the theme that in and

of ourselves we are truly incapable of comprehending in any detailed way how God works in either creating or permitting suffering in this world. Strictly speaking, much suffering is simply unintelligible. There are no persuasive teleological explanations available.

In our resistance against this conclusion it is tempting to think of Job's encounter with God at the end as a form of explanation that somehow should bring a measure of intellectual relief. Eleonore Stump, in one of the most penetrating readings of Job to appear in decades, would appear to think that this is the case. Stump rejects the possibility of a teleological explanation of Job's suffering. This would represent a third-person account of what is going on in the life of Job. Instead we should think of a second-person account of what is happening, that is, an account embodied in a story that gives us access to the interactions of agents involved in an intimate and personal relationship. Such a story "gives a person some of what she would have had if she had unmediated personal interaction with the characters of the story while they were conscious and interacting with each other." What is available is Franciscan knowledge rather than Dominican knowledge. The latter is knowledge that, expressed in propositions, states that this or that is the case; the former is knowledge of persons, knowledge not reducible to propositions, but captured in stories that give us access to the knowledge irreducibly transmitted from one person to another. This switch of perspective means that we can say that "Job gets what he wants in the story—namely, an explanation of why he suffers."[1]

Stump supplies a graphic analogy to bring home what she means. She asks us to consider a mother who has a child suffering the horrible pains of a bone marrow transplant because of aggressive leukemia. She might try to comfort him by explaining the medical procedures needed to replace unhealthy cells with healthy ones. Stump then writes:

> This might be the right explanation for the son in the hospital, but then again it might not be. There are circumstances in which the third-explanations of this sort are inefficacious for comfort. The child undergoing a painful medical procedure may be less frightened and hurt by what he takes to be his mother's abandonment of him, her apparent indifference to his pain and need, as by anything that is happening to his bones and mucus membranes. In that case, the best response to his need for an explanation—perhaps the only response that makes love bio-available to him—is for the mother to give her son a second-person experience of her as loving him. This may be the best means in the circumstances to show him that she would only let him suffer in order to bring about some outweighing good for him that she could not get for him in any easier way. In cases in which an apparent betrayal of trust is an important part of suffering, second-person explanations have a special power to console. There is a particularly potent comfort in Job in the second-person explanation he gets in the narrative. Certainly, it is more intense for him than a third-person account could be.[2]

Stump adds the interesting observation that God honors Job in restoration, but this happily does not affect what has to be said immediately in response to her perceptive reading of Job. What has to be said is that Job's experience of God face to face in no way involves an explanation of what he has been through. There is not even the hint of an outweighing good that God could not give him in any easier way. In speaking in this way, Stump falls back into the standard language of explanation where God allows or brings about this or that suffering in order to bring about some good not otherwise possible. As she rightly points out, what Job gets is consolation and restoration. Neither of these supplies anything by way of serious explanation. Indeed the point of the preceding confession by Job is that he does not have a clue as to how to explain what God is doing; it is strictly outside his capacities as a finite creature.

There is a more fitting way to think of what is going on in appeal to divine encounter. In meeting God face to face, Job does not have an explanation, but he does know God now in a way he did not know God before. We might think of Job as an old-fashioned Methodist who has met God face to face and thus has moved from an inherited faith of tradition and transmission to one of personal knowledge. It is this personal acquaintance with God that outweighs the counterevidence that he has endured in the calamities that have befallen him. To be sure, the chastening of his intellectual pretensions plays its part in weakening any quick and easy path from suffering to any conclusion about what God is doing and thus challenging the standing attributes of God as revealed in creation and redemption. However, the brevity of the reference to encounter with God should not be allowed to gauge its significance. Job is returning to a vital component of his Jewish theology where God is met face to face and where he leaves the encounter with as many questions as he had before. Indeed, the encounter with God as exhibited by earlier witnesses like Moses and Isaiah brings with it its own raft of darkness and perplexity. Yet such darkness and perplexity do not for a moment undercut the weight that such encounter bears in the structure of faith; it is a crucial warrant for continuing to trust God even if God kills him, over against cursing God or abandoning the God of Israel for the tempting pastures of polytheism, atheism, or the other options available in the public square.

In closing, I would like to highlight some of the issues covered and add an observation or two on the significance of incomprehensibility for the life of the mind for a mature believer.

The treatment of suffering in the book of Job throws light on a host of issues we commonly and rightly associate with suffering. Suffering comes in various shapes and sizes, from social and political turmoil and folly, from natural disasters, and from personal disease. Suffering is often psychologically devastating. We need consolation and help from others. Merely getting through can be as important as final deliverance and relief; mere grinning and bearing can be a form of success, for divine intervention does not always happen. Yet genuine recovery is possible. Suffering can lead to recognition of our finite understanding of creation and the ways of God. It can also be the occasion for a deeper encounter with God and thus with a stronger and more robust faith in God. It can be the occasion rather than the reason for the maturing of a naïve faith in divine providence.

Suffering is not, however, essential to a deep faith in God. Interestingly, Job figures as a paradigm of patience in the only reference to him in the New Testament; he is not the prime candidate as the paradigm of faith. That coveted place belongs to Abraham. Compared to Job, Abraham's life was relatively easy. Moreover, our Lord makes clear that another paradigm of true faith is children, and in that context there is no reference to suffering whatsoever. This is not to say that as followers of Christ we are not subject to suffering, for we are. Indeed Paul makes the startling statement that he desires to be conformed to Christ in his death. Insofar as I have followed this theme where it shows up, that is, in his epistle to the Philippians, Paul appears to mean by this the readiness to bear the suffering that comes from following Christ in a crooked and perverse generation. This dovetails with the whole theme of cross-bearing so central to disciple-ship in the Gospels. Such suffering is not the kind identified in Job but the suffering that comes from bearing the offense of Christ in a world that has lost its bearings in creation and redemption. To be sure, we can readily offer up any and all suffering to God that he may use it for his glory, as the great saints have done across the ages. However, none of these observations show that suffering is essential to a strong and mighty faith in God. They exhibit strong faith; they are not a necessary condition of strong faith.

Furthermore, the incomprehensibility of much suffering is not a license to eschew the pursuit of theodicy, that is, the effort to justify some of the ways of God as they relate to suffering as we speak to ourselves and to our critics. This is the wrong inference fideists are tempted to take from the story of Job. Once we take a wider walk through the canon of scripture we find all sorts of efforts to understand suffering as it relates to divine action. Think of the story of Joseph; or the theme of the suffering servant in Isaiah; or the man-ifold attempts to make sense of the suffering of Christ for the redemption of the world in theories of the atonement. More generally, this way of thinking undercuts the whole enterprise of theology itself; for much of theology, if not the heart of theology, is to make sense of the complex network of divine actions displayed in creation and redemption. The confession of inescapable ignorance that cannot be avoided in theology is no excuse for laying down our tools and giving up on our trade. The fact that we do not have complete explanations does not for a moment entail that we do not have good partial explanations. Half a theological loaf is better than no bread at all.

The fact of the matter is that comprehensibility eludes us when we come to the blessings of God every bit as much as when we come to the providence of God in suffering and disaster. We have no explanation as to why God should choose Abram and the Jews to be the bearers of his blessings to the whole world. God's coming to us in the incarnation is a matter of stupendous surprise; it is not something we would readily predicate of divine grace and love. God's saving the world through the death of his Son is as much an offense today as it was originally. The workings of God in our lives as he brings liberation to the world can be post factum charted; they are not obviously explicable in and of themselves. God's choice of what is weak in the world to confound the wise of the world is surely not something precisionist analytic philosophers would even begin to posit as a way to bring salvation to the world.

So it is with the blessings of the world to come. The writer of Job notes at the end that Job is approved by God and is then restored to an abundance of prosperity even greater than he had enjoyed before. To the wise of this world, this comes off as a fairy tale, a story with a happy ending to help the children sleep at night after the nightmare of his suffering. This is not so for the mature believer who has come to terms with the gospel and become immersed in the canonical faith of the church. The fundamental issue is that of divine approval; the restoration and reward are the icing on the cake. In a brilliant sermon, C. S. Lewis captures the issue of approval in this fashion.

> In the end the Face which is the delight or terror of the universe must be turned upon us either with one expression or with the other, either conferring glory inexpressible or inflicting shame that can never be cured or disguised. I read in a periodical the other day that the fundamental thing is how we think of God. By God Himself, it is not! How God thinks of us is not only more important, but infinitely more important. Indeed, how we think of Him is of no importance except in so far as it is related to how He thinks of us. It is written that we shall "stand before" Him, shall appear, shall be inspected. The promise of glory is the promise, almost incredible and only possible by the work of Christ, that some of us, that any of us who really chooses, shall actually survive that examination, shall find approval, shall please God. To please God . . . to be a real ingredient in the divine happiness . . . to be loved by God, not merely pitied, but delighted in as an artist delights in his work or a father delights in a son . . . it seems impossible, a weight or burden of glory which our thoughts can hardly sustain. But so it is.[3]

As with Job, the first issue of business in the matter is divine approval. Restoration and glory follow as one more amazing gift bestowed upon us. The restoration and glory will come to us finally not in this life, as was the case with Job, but in the world to come. "You show me the path of life. In your presence there is fullness of joy; in your right hand are pleasures forevermore" (Ps. 16:11).

CHAPTER 5

Death and the Death of Christ

Seeking to understand death and the suffering that it can evoke is not for the faint of heart. Yet nowhere has the challenge been more acute for me than when I sought to relate the suffering brought about by the death of my beloved Timothy to the suffering and death of Christ. When I first began to organize my thoughts in an orderly fashion, my initial intuition was that the connections would be so obvious that there would be little to worry about. Indeed the problem seemed to be this: surely there will be so many connections to pursue that the difficulty will simply be one of selection and subsequent articulation. I could not have been more wrong. Sorting through my journey on this front will begin to explain why this has been the case.

Initially I was taken by the extraordinary remark of Paul in the middle of his letter to the Philippians.

> I regard everything as loss because of the surpassing value of knowing Christ Jesus my Lord. For his sake I have suffered the loss of all things, and I regard them as rub-

bish, in order that I may gain Christ and be found in him, not having a righteousness of my own that comes from the law, but one that comes through faith in Christ, the righteousness from God based on faith. I want to know Christ and the power of his resurrection and *the sharing of his sufferings by becoming like him in his death*, if somehow I may attain the resurrection from the dead. (Phil. 3:8–14)

Surely, I thought, this was an obvious text to ponder given the issue at hand. Here was an astonishing text that sandwiched the theme of suffering in between the victory achieved in Christ's resurrection and our ultimate resurrection from the dead. Moreover, it was a text that related the theme of suffering directly to the theme of the death of Christ. Yet my hopes were quickly dashed. I found myself riveted by the desire on the part of Paul to take suffering as represented by the death of Christ as something to be sought with such intensity. Taken in isolation, this comes across as hopelessly masochistic. Who in their right mind would want to seek out suffering modeled on the death of Christ as a pivotal element in their scheme of values? Surely, suffering is something we desire to come to an end! Even so, the oddity of this desire caught my attention. Here was a strange comment about suffering that turns our normal ways of thinking upside down. Rather than running away from suffering or trying to diminish suffering as much as possible, Paul was embracing it with enthusiasm. How could this be? Could there be a connection between the suffering brought about by deep grief and the suffering identified here? In order to pursue this I immediately decided to work my way through the whole letter to the Philippians in search of an answer. To be honest, I was not given any help at all.

The letter, of course, has much to say about suffering. Thus it develops the theme of the suffering of Paul, the suffering of the Philippian Christians, and the suffering of Christ. It is obvious that Paul provides sterling pastoral wisdom in pointing out that all three agents here have this in common: they all fell afoul of systematic persecution that resulted in suffering for their commitment to God. Just as Christ was steadfast in his obedience even to death, so Paul too intended to remain faithful to death in following Christ in his vocation, and thus his own example provided both warrant and motivation for faithful disciples in Philippi to do the same. He owed so much to Christ's obedience in securing a whole new way of relating by faith to God, that psychologically there was really no alternative to staying the course and suffering whatever might befall him. Moreover, the death of Christ was followed by the victory of his resurrection. In knowing Christ one came to know the same power that raised Christ from the dead; and in God's good time Paul's suffering too would lead to his own resurrection from the dead. The same promise was implicitly held out to the suffering faithful in Philippi.

This is frankly irrelevant to those going through deep suffering brought about by the death of a loved one. In Paul's case the suffering is due to persecution; in grieving over a loved one the cause of suffering is not persecution but simply the terrible loss of a loved one. In Paul's case—as indeed in the case of Christ and the Philippians—the suffering is avoidable and entirely voluntary. In the case of grief the suffering is absolutely unavoidable; it simply hits one in waves where there is no choice in the matter. In Paul's case, the suffering involved makes sense in a world hostile to the gospel and the will of God; it is entirely explicable that folk who detest the moral and spiritual challenge represented by Christ will seek to eliminate it; by extension this same logic makes sense of persecution of Christ's disciples. In the case of deep grief the suffering can be so intense that the very idea of looking for an explanation can be acutely insensitive. Put simply, we are dealing with two radically different kinds of suffering: the suffering of the martyr over against the natural suffering that can hit believer and unbeliever as a bolt from the blue. To be sure, one can readily reach for an analogy. Just as we can offer up to God the suffering that arises because of the hostility of others to our faith and ask God to use it and redeem it, so too can we offer up the suffering that arises from grief and ask God to use it and redeem it. Anyone committed to a serious doctrine of providence will insist on this. However, analogy is not identity; it is pious nonsense to wish away the crucial differences just enumerated.

Clearly, the connection between suffering due to grief and suffering due to persecution and opposition are sufficiently different that it is unwise to relate them directly to the suffering manifest in the death of Christ. Yet surely there is an obvious connection when we look at the suffering of Christ in the face of death represented by Jesus in his response to the death of Lazarus and represented by his anticipation of his own death. In the one case the suffering is retrospective and in the other prospective. In the case of Lazarus, Jesus weeps at his tomb. In the case of his own death we are confronted with the agony of Gethsemane. Here surely is precisely the kind of material that deserves our closest attention. The challenge, of course, is to interpret this material accurately and sensitively.

One natural way to proceed is to see in the weeping over the death of Lazarus the same sense of loss that we all feel at the loss of a dear friend. However, it has been common to go beyond this and see in the grief of Jesus a sense of anger at the reality of death. What is at issue, it will be said, is something much deeper than natural grief; what is at issue is an understanding of death as our last enemy that needs to be defeated. Death is seen as an intrusion into creation; it is a ghastly interruption that should be seen for what it is, that is, as an enemy. In speaking of death as an enemy that rightly evokes emotions of grief and anger, we are deploying a crucial text of Paul where precisely this language is used. Thus: "The last enemy to be destroyed is death" (1 Cor. 15:26). The context is one where Paul announces that in the resurrection of Christ God has already begun to subject the fallen creation to a redemption already initiated in Christ but waiting to be completed in the future.

> But in fact Christ has been raised from the dead, the first fruits of those who have died. For since death came through a human being, the resurrection of the dead has also come through a human being; for as all die in Adam, so all will be made alive in Christ. But each in his own order: Christ the first fruits, then at his coming those who belong to Christ. Then comes the end, when he hands over the kingdom to God the Father, after he has destroyed every ruler and every authority and power. For he must reign until he has put all his enemies under his feet. The last enemy to be destroyed is death. (1 Cor. 15:20–26)

What is at issue here is a range of theological themes that have evoked extended commentary in systematic theology, ranging from the claim that physical death follows as a consequence of Adam's sin to the claim that Christ's resurrection is a critical first step in the defeat of physical death in a journey that will end with our resurrection from the dead. The critical issue at stake in the current discussion is the claim that death is an enemy that cries out to be defeated. It is not, therefore, something we should naturally welcome. We should see it as something alien and foreign, something to be treated with contempt and disdain. Thus we should see our grief and even our anger in the face of death as something entirely fitting. On this analysis our grief is a correct intellectual reading of the situation: we are faced in the death of a loved one with the stark reality of death as an enemy that has gained a temporary victory in our lives. In the end, death will indeed be defeated; however, in this life, this is not yet the case; death remains an enemy that rightly evokes grief and anger when we meet it in the death of our loved ones. We should therefore expect to mourn our sense of loss. We have been confronted with an enemy who has temporarily crushed and overwhelmed us. It is only right then that we should grieve and lament our loss. This is not mere psychological reaction; it bespeaks, it is argued, a deep theological intuition that registers a profound insight into the nature of reality. Our looking back in joy at the victory of Christ over death and our looking forward in hope at our own resurrection from the dead cannot undo the stark reality of death as an enemy. Any kind of shallow optimism is shattered by the rude awakening to reality represented by the death of our nearest and dearest. This is clearly a very fertile line of investigation, and I shall return to echoes of this way of dealing with death before I finish.

Note immediately that this whole way of thinking is, of course, bizarre to those who reject a robust Christian understanding of reality. Moreover, we have left behind the thin resources of deism and mere theism and crossed over the threshold into the robust content of the Christian tradition. This change in perspective mirrors an important shift in the recent literature on the problem of evil. While there remains a wealth of material on the problem of suffering as a problem for all forms of generic theism, the turn to the internal content of Christian theology as a resource for dealing with the problem of evil represented by suffering is a refreshing development. At one level it is in line with the extraordinary renewal of work on the great themes of Christian theology; at another level it is a much-needed breakthrough for students of philosophy who have grown tired of the conventional rounds of debate about natural theology and miracles in the standard textbooks. Yet we must keep our wits about us and make sure that the proposals developed get the critical scrutiny they deserve. We know from our experience with traditional debates within theodicy that the arena is littered with false promises; perhaps it should not surprise us if the same happens with the promises offered in more recent theology. In order to pursue this possibility let us look at two ways of thinking through how the experience of the death of a loved one might be connected in a deep way to the death of Christ.

Consider first some crucial features of the remarkable proposal laid out with exquisite care in the recent work of Marilyn McCord Adams.[1] Adams's work is excruciatingly forthright in her insistence that we take with radical seriousness the horrors that befall us. She knows the standard moves in theodicy that seek to justify the ways of God and not unnaturally finds them inadequate, not least because they do not face the full force of the range of evil and suffering we encounter. She insists that the acute problem represented by horrors is that they can undermine our sense of meaning. Horrendous evils do not just involve appalling suffering, they dehumanize us; they break our wills, degrade us, disorient us, and deprive us of the possibility of ascribing positive personal meaning to our lives. Things are so bad, in fact, that we are incapable of conceiving how far we are complicit in personal and collective participation in countless forms of horror. Efforts at justifying the ways of God in such circumstances fail because God is responsible for the wider causal web of events in which our actions are enmeshed. Even so, the whole idea of justifying the ways of God is a priori misleading because "God has no obligations to creatures and hence no need to *justify* divine actions to us."[2] Hence we need to rethink the network of issues involved from top to bottom. This is precisely what Adams sets out to do.

My focus here is on how we might connect the suffering involved in acute grief with the death of Christ, so I set aside any large-scale evaluation of the depth and range of Adams's proposals and keep my exposition severely within limits. To begin we must reckon with the massive metaphysical size-gap she posits between God and human creatures. God's ways are higher than our ways, so communication from the divine side is difficult and trust on our end is hard to win. Yet, she insists, we can still sketch relatively robustly the ways of God and begin to relate them to the destruction of personal meaning that horrors inevitably engender.

The story runs something like this. God loves material reality; we can see this immediately from the story of the incarnation. Indeed the primary reason for the creation of the material world was to provide for the possibility of such an intimate union with material reality. "*God creates this world because God wants to be Christ for a material world such as this!*"[3] The snag of course is that, given what we know from evolution and how our world has come into being, this means that we human agents are subject to vulnerability. God's desire to personify material reality and thus create embodied agents makes us Godlike. However, it also sets us up for disaster in that it makes us radically vulnerable to horrors and thus prima facie deprives our lives of positive meaning. We are doomed to prima facie ruination. Not to worry, however, for God addresses this predicament by becoming united with our nature in the hypostatic union so carefully spelled out in classical Christian thinking in the patristic and medieval world. God engages in an act of radical solidarity with us; God enters into the world of horrors that has emerged, given his love for material reality. Thus God participates in the horrors that are built into creation, defeating them in the life and death of Christ, and thereafter inviting us into an intimate personal and corporate relation with the risen Christ in the church, so that we may feed on him intimately in his presence in the Eucharist, work through the defeat of meaning in this life and the life to come, and finally reach an afterlife in which everyone shares in the life of God in such a manner that we can integrate the suffering we endured into an account of our lives that we recognize as positively meaningful. In the end we shall be able to recognize that the horrors we have endured do not undermine a positive vision of the meaning of our lives. This is made possible in the life of Christ and its aftermath; moreover, the victory of Christ over horrors and the ensuing threat to meaning is such that everybody eventually can confess and embrace the effects of Christ's life and work for themselves.

We can see what is going on here relatively easily. Adams reconstructs the Christian story of creation and redemption in order to address the problem of the loss of meaning occasioned by our experience of horrors rather than the problem of sin. She retells the story of Christ as a story of victory of his own struggles with horrors brought about by his opponents and by his own unwilling but real participation in the production of horrors. She refigures the standard vision of the church and Eucharist as a place of healing in which we can participate in Christ's victory over the potential loss of meaning. She recasts the themes of personal and cosmic eschatology by reworking a vision of purgatory and ultimate universal salvation. Given her initial vision of the metaphysical size-gap between ourselves and God, the final reunion with God in the eschaton is more than enough to heal us from our loss of meaning in the face of suffering and to provide adequate compensation for what we have endured in order for God to have the kind of material world that set the whole cosmos in motion at the outset. The sweep of her thinking and the range of philosophical skill on display are simply breathtaking.

The crucial question here is how this fascinating reworking of Christian theology might address the problem of acute suffering brought about by the death of a loved one. To be sure, this may appear trivial in the face of the catalogue of horrors developed by Adams. However, the particularities of suffering matter. If the proposed solution does not deliver in this more modest case, it is not clear how it might deliver in more dramatic cases.

Much hinges initially on what one makes of the remarkable story told with such skill by Adams. Leave aside for the moment the initial account of the human predicament as involving the problem of meaning rather than the problem of sin. Leave aside also the crucial premise that divine creation necessarily involves subjecting human agents to horrendous horrors given our creaturely vulnerability. Leave aside in addition the claim that we are in no position to ask God to provide a justification for divine actions, as if this principle holds once God sets creation as envisaged in motion; or better still, as if the quest to find reasons for divine actions is somehow not a form of seeking for relevant justifications for divine action; and as if divine revelation does not give us partial insight into why God does what God does.

The deeper issues are these. First, the idea that God offers himself as a sacrifice to us for putting us through the misery we face is ludicrous on its face. Equally bizarre is the claim that we get to take our anger out on God by rejecting and crucifying the Son of God. Adams takes up this notion afresh when she explains her vision of the Eucharist in terms of impanation. In a way parallel to the union between divine and human natures in Christ, there is an equally robust union between Christ and the bread and wine. Thus we get to chomp and bite on Christ and return horrors for horrors on a weekly basis. Of course, there is more to the Eucharist than this, for it is also an occasion for thanksgiving to Christ and for intimate fellowship with Christ. However, surely something has gone badly wrong with the proposal if paying God back for what God has inflicted on us in this sacred meal is even a live option for us.

Second, while it is certainly relevant to note that God has entered into the suffering of the world in a deep way, we need care in unpacking what is at stake. I say this not to resolve the thorny debates about impassibility and immutability but to note that Adams cautiously accepts the notion that somehow God feels our pain both in our present suffering and in entering into the mind-blowing experience of Christ in the crucifixion. In the former case we run into the problem of radical incoherence in our conception of the divine. If God somehow feels everyone's pain, then God is enduring horrendous pain all the time. That in itself is enough to make things worse rather than better; we are now told that our suffering is multiplied ad nauseam in the life of God. But there is worse to ponder. If God feels our pain, does God not also feel our pleasures? If so, we have a divine agent who is, to put it sharply, in need of our pity and sorrow and whose internal disposition (if we can use this language) is utterly incoherent. We are driven to think of God as at once the subject of horrendous pain and exquisite bliss. In the latter case, that is, the appeal to the experience of Christ, surely there are more apt ways of thinking of the suffering of Christ, say, in Gethsemane, that take far more seriously the deep sense of confidence in God that pervades the passion stories. Even so in the case of acute grief, being told that God feels our current pain or that Christ had temporally lost his grip on the meaning of his life is every bit as useless as being told just-so stories about why God permits the suffering that befalls us. Given the utter darkness into which we descend, it is difficult to see how this will bring either illumination or consolation.

Perhaps I have missed something here. Maybe Adams is claiming not that there is consolation here but that later by the grace and power of God we will be able to construe this in such a way that it is integrated into a positive story of the meaning of our lives. However, this way of thinking is wide of the mark because to speak in this way is a serious misreading of our situation. Thus we come to a third consideration. What hits us is not so much the loss of meaning; it is the loss of our beloved son. On the contrary, there may be no loss of the wider sense of meaning in terms of creation, providence, the love of God for us, and the like. Nor need there be any sense of anger that would drive us to want to hit back at God and go to church and bite and chomp on his body and blood. What is at issue is much more mundane; our beloved child has died and we desperately want him back so we can continue our fragile lives together. More needs to be said here both about the impact of death and the absence or loss of meaning. The crucial point is simple: like the women at the tomb, we have lost a dear one and are overwhelmed with grief. Loss of meaning is not the primary issue; it is a secondary issue. The crucial initial issue is the stark reality of death itself and the immediate effect the loss has on our lives.

At this point it is appropriate to pick up the thread I left dangling earlier when I began to unpack a much more traditional vision of death that starts from the stark reality of death itself and seeks to provide an account of death as the last enemy to be defeated. This is a proposal that has received extended treatment by the distinguished Orthodox theologian David Bentley Hart.[4] Strains of his work can also be found in the work of Alexander Schmemann,[5] but I will restrict my review to that provided by Hart.

Hart shares with Adams a radical sense of realism when it comes to the depths of human suffering. In dealing with the horrendous tsunami that struck offshore of Banda Aceh at the northern end of Sumatra in 2004 he deploys his comprehensive rhetorical skill and resources to bring home the depths of human suffering. In this respect his great hero is Voltaire, who, in describing the Lisbon earthquake of 1755, excoriated those philosophers who had sought to provide the standard forms of theodicy long known in the literature. Hart's contempt for contemporary analytic philosophers is more than a match for the vitriol of Voltaire against figures like Leibniz. Vile intellectual creatures that they are, they reduce "God to a finite ethical agent, a limited psychological personality, whose purposes are measurable upon the same scale as ours, and whose ultimate ends for his creatures do not transcend the cosmos as we perceive it."[6] Moreover, they and those Christians who try to answer the standard questions on the problem of evil and suffering systematically ignore the internal content of the Christian faith. Worse still, they fail to see that even though providence means that God can bring good out of suffering and death, the New Testament "teaches us that, in another and ultimate sense, suffering and death—considered in themselves—have no true meaning or purpose at all; and this is the most liberating and joyous wisdom that the gospel imparts" (35). It looks as if Hart has raised the stakes at this point. We are told that the very absence of meaning and purpose as far as suffering and death are concerned is somehow a form of liberating and joyous wisdom that is imparted by the gospel. Presumably this is where the content of the Christian faith makes a radical difference to our thinking. On the face of it, this claim is absurd. However, let's not move too fast.

Hart spells this out with his inimitable rhetorical skill. In the end his account will take us to the empty tomb, an event that "has shattered the heart of nature and history alike (as we [Christians] understand them) and fashioned them anew" (44). What we have is his alternative and more standard reading of the Christian narrative of creation, freedom, fall, and redemption.

Looking aright at creation we can revere the God made manifest in its varied beauties of meadows, mountains, seas, and stars. This is a matter not of inference but of perception. Yet we can also see the omnipresence of death. "It is as if the entire cosmos were somehow predatory, a single great organism nourishing itself upon the death of everything to which it gives birth, creating and devouring all things with a terrible and impassive majesty" (50). Seen merely as nature or as the premise for a natural theology, this observation will lead us to see a deity whose power and will are constrained by certain logical possibilities, or perhaps lead us to a monstrous deity driven by inscrutable malice, or perhaps bring us to a deity who is a glorious Absolute enjoined to a world of horrific sacrifice as manifest in a war where millions perish. Hart will have none of these, for he thinks a Christian vision of the world provides a better alternative.

In that vision God is goodness itself. God is infinite truth and beauty, the source and end of all things, the infinite wellspring of all being. "Thus everything that comes from God must be good and true and beautiful" (55). We are bidden to behold God's love and goodness in all of the created order. In the language of Thomas Traherne, the world is "the Paradise of God" (57). To see this one must approach it with "an eye rendered limpid by love" (60). To be sure, we can see it as nature, that is, as a world marked by beauty and terror, by delight and dreariness. However, the world is not mere nature; it is a creation that exhibits an endless sea of glory, radiant with the beauty of God. Through the veil of death we see creation as something beautiful. The evil we behold in suffering and death is a radically negative world in the sense that it is even worse than the standard works on theodicy depict it. Yet it can also be seen as a world of cosmic contingencies, ontological shadows, intrinsically devoid of substance or purpose. It is thus negative in a more metaphysical sense in that it really amounts to a privation of the good, "a purely parasitic corruption of the created reality, possessing no essence or nature of its own" (73).

This is surely a puzzling if not incoherent set of observations about the world. Because they are decked out in the costume of a venerable theological tradition and put on display with the vast store of semantic and rhetorical power with which Hart is equipped, it is easy to be distracted and intellectually manipulated into submission. We should not be fooled and distracted by Hart's intellectually superficial and intemperate treatment of the traditional worries that crop up in the literature on theodicy and the problem of evil. This polemical sideshow cannot hide the fact that his high-octane metaphysical claims simply do not match the veridical grip of the observations that Hart himself invites the reader to perceive and ponder. We cannot dispose of our ordinary perceptions of death, suffering, and evil so cavalierly. We are dealing with real causal agents, not some sort of shadowy realities that somehow lack ontological weight in their own right. Even Hart has to admit that even as they depend on God, they have deep causal efficacy at the level of our persistent observation of the way things are, and subsequently at the level of the deep intuitions these observations naturally sustain. Indeed their very dependence on God represented in traditional doctrines of divine preservation and concurrence implicates God in the damage, death, and suffering we experience.

One senses that Hart is fully aware of all this, for he insists on deploying other dimensions of the Christian tradition to fill out his theological narrative. Thus he takes very seriously the reality of human agency as representing a world of genuine human freedom. Equally, he boldly insists on the reality of the demonic as an undeniable feature of the world we inhabit.

> In the New Testament, our condition as fallen creatures
> is explicitly portrayed as a subjugation to the subsidiary
> and often mutinous authority of angelic and demonic
> "powers," which are not able to defeat God's transcen-
> dent and providential governance of all things but which
> certainly are able to act against him within the cosmic
> limits of time. (65)

These would not appear to be mere shadows of reality, mere
epiphenomena thrown up by a deeper reality. Indeed at this
point, Hart deploys the traditional notion of an initial catastrophe, an initial fall within creation, which leads to the
introduction of death as a mortal enemy that has to be defeated. The resolution of this catastrophe is to be found in the
glorious victory over death and evil that is represented by the
empty tomb. We face in Christ's resurrection a plenitude of
charity that steps into human history in the incarnation "to
subvert death and to provide a way through to a new life" (81).
Thus Easter reverses the verdict that has been pronounced
against Christ, confounds the rulers of this age, and emanci-
pates us from servitude to terror before the elements of the
world. In this there is absolutely no hint of God needing to
offer some kind of sacrifice to us for our enduring the horrors
tied to God's love for a material world. Nor for that matter is
there any idea that either in the crucifixion or in the Eucharist we can express our anger and resentment toward God for
having to suffer ruination due to the inescapable vulnerability of our horror-stricken existence ultimately inflicted upon
us by God in creation. Given the utter fecundity of divine
goodness and love, these kinds of moves are ludicrous if not
blasphemous. The crucial issue is that death is an enemy that
arises because of an original catastrophe and rebellion that

lies at the heart of creation. Death thus understood has been defeated once for all in the death and resurrection of Christ. A genuinely Easter faith calls upon us to recognize the horror that it is and rise up in rebellion against it through the victory won by Christ. Joined to Christ, we can now yield ourselves in love in union with God. We do not need to look at death or suffering as something brought about directly by God or planned by God to achieve some hidden plan within the created order.

How might this relate to the unbearable grief we experience at the death of a loved one? Hart speaks directly and poignantly to this issue. He tells the story of a father in Sri Lanka. The father was

> a large man of enormous physical strength who was unable to prevent four of his five children from perishing in the tsunami, and who—as he recited the names of his lost children to the reporter, ending with the name of his four-year-old son—was utterly overwhelmed by his own weeping. Only a moral cretin at that moment would have attempted to soothe his anguish by assuring him that his children had died as a result of God's eternal, inscrutable, and righteous counsels, and that in fact their deaths have mysteriously served God's purposes in history and that all this was completely necessary to God to accomplish his ultimate design in having created a world. (99–100)

To speak in such a manner would be a matter of vile stupidity; it would be a lie told for our own comfort.

> In the process, moreover, we would be attempting to deny that man a knowledge central to the gospel: the knowledge of the evil in death, its intrinsic falsity, its unjust

102

dominion over the world, its ultimate nullity: the knowledge that God is not pleased or nourished by our deaths, that he is not the secret architect of evil, that he is the conqueror of hell, that he has condemned all these things by the power of his cross; the knowledge that God is life and light and infinite love, and the path that leads through nature and history to his Kingdom does not simply follow the contours of either nature or history, or obey the logic immanent to them, but is opened to us by way of the natural and historical absurdity—or outrage—of the empty tomb. (100-101)

All this is magnificently said, but what are we to make of it? Initially the level of honesty is refreshing in the extreme. Yet we have to pause. Thinking of the death of a child, Hart says this: "As for comfort when we seek it, I can imagine none greater than the happy knowledge that when I see the death of a child, I do not see the face of God but the face of his enemy" (103-4). I can only respond that I cannot but read this as a piece of pious nonsense. It is a futile attempt to replace the pieties of traditional theodicies with the pieties of a robust but obscurantist understanding of the world. There is no such comfort in claims like this; they fail to do justice to the depths of our misery and agony. To be sure, we can qualify the claim and say that initially, given our grief, nothing will comfort us in our sorrow. When we regain our reflective capacities it is a claim like this, it is hoped, that will assuage our cognitive dissonance. However, this only works if the supporting narrative is persuasive.

It is not persuasive for the following reason. If we see death as the result of an original catastrophe or fall, then either it has been inflicted on us by the demonic—the claim

Hart would appear to support—or it has been inflicted upon us by God as a punishment for sin. The former is simply nonsense given our standard and proper causal accounts of death as we meet it in real life. Death is not due to the intervention of the demonic, however we might conceive the agency of the demonic in relation to natural causes. The latter alternative on the other hand surely insists that death is something we should morally welcome, for, on this analysis, we deserve death as the punishment for our sin either originally or as an appropriate response of God to our persistent human waywardness. If we construe it as an enemy we must then see God as our enemy in the encounter with death. Yet this is precisely what Hart is at pains to disallow. What we effectively have here is the old theological parlor trick of holding on to the conclusions of an earlier theological argument when the premises have been systematically eroded and set aside. Even then, the tradition by no means insisted that physical death is the result of sin. John Wesley rejected this whole line of argument on the grounds that Adam lived for nine hundred years before he died.[7] What was really at issue was spiritual death, a move picked up in treatments that see death as an enemy in terms of the personification of Death as symbolic of the disastrous moral and spiritual consequence for our rebellion against God. Given spiritual death, then one consequence of this was fear of death, not death itself, a move that has at least the initial merit of not being prima facie fallacious.

The upshot of our review of two influential efforts to deal with the problem of grief in the face of death and of the stark reality of death is this: appeals to the internal content of Christian theology do not deliver on the promises offered. This is not to deny the need to explore both traditional and revisionist accounts of Christian theology in order to find intellectual solace and illumination. I leave it to others to outwit the proposals developed by Hart and Adams. For my part I bring this little exercise to a conclusion by revisiting three central claims that have recurred in the course of my deliberations.

First, there is no persuasive theological rationale for much of the suffering we have to endure. Initially, such suffering naturally leads to the overwhelming of our cognitive capacities so that neither our central beliefs nor our attempts at theological explanation offer any kind of direct consolation. Perhaps the best explanation of our grief and suffering is the simplest: we suffer because we love; and when we lose a beloved child, the measure of our grief and our darkness is the measure of our love. It would be easy to dismiss this as sentimental prattle; I consider it to be a profound platitude.

Second, it is natural given the riches of our faith and the ingenuity of our speculative intellects to look for more. For my part I remain a radically skeptical Christian theist who believes that the glories prepared for us in the life to come are ultimately beyond our comprehension. This is matched by the parallel conviction that the reasons for the range and depth of our suffering are equally beyond our comprehension. This is not an invitation to abandon the quest for relevant explanations, much less to score cheap rhetorical points against such work either in philosophy or theology. Questions remain to haunt us, and it is simply silly to try to deny them or to bully us into rejecting them with spurious arguments. Moreover, my radical skepticism is a hard-won conviction gained across the years; it is not the starting point of the discussion; it is a settled conviction after years of pondering the relevant issues.

Third, there is no going back on the crucial Christian claim that the life, death, and resurrection of Christ have a decisive bearing on our understanding and experience of the reality of death. The death of Christ as an atoning sacrifice for the sins of the whole world is a precious truth that has significant ramifications for our lives and for our deaths. At the very least, this means that we approach the death of our loved ones in a way that is different from those who do not share this deep truth of the gospel. Even so, it is simply not the case that this difference means that we do not enter the devastating world of grief experienced in the death of a loved one. There is a weight and gravity to that grief that cannot be relieved; we have to walk through that valley as courageously and firmly as we can.

Fourth, in the Christian life of suffering we walk by faith and not by sight. Given the combined weight of divine revelation, of the experience of the love of God, of the reality of conspicuous sanctity, and of our perception of divine agency in the natural world, we have more than enough to secure the life of discipleship. Moreover, the whole story of creation, freedom, sin, providence, and redemption supplies its own illuminating resources even as it provokes a whole new network of questions and puzzles. We can add to this the inescapable note of victory over suffering and death in the person and work of Christ and the extraordinary promises held forth in the gospel. In the midst of our grief and loss, these considerations are present in our minds, but they do not function as they do when we recover our equilibrium and face a future where the absence is always present. In our grief, we are coming to terms with our loves. These loves are indeed an echo of a greater Love that embraces us all and that is given to us in Christ. Yet these lesser loves have their own inimitable place in our hearts and minds; I, for one, would never want to have it otherwise.

Notes

Notes to Chapter 1

1. *Representative Verse of Charles Wesley*, ed. Frank Baker (Nashville: Abingdon, 1962), 280.

2. Other than by reference here or there in the notes I will not deal with the following issues that crop up more generally in debates about divine healing. I will not deal with the claim that miracles have ceased since the closing of the canon of scripture; the challenge posed by scientific investigation and often identified as the problem of the "God of the gaps"; the distinction between miracles understood as divine acts that involve "violations of a law of nature" and divine miraculous acts understood as miracles of coincidence; the epistemological challenge of providing warrants for claims about divine healing; and the challenge of how to relate the miraculous acts of God to divine action in creation.

3. Another way to put the liberal Protestant option is to say that God operates on the basis of a general policy of nonintervention.

4. One way to describe the dispensationalist evangelical option is to say that God operated in the past by means of divine intervention but not today. Often this is referred to as the cessationist position, a position also held by B. B. Warfield in the nineteenth century.

5. There are clearly circumstances in which deep experience of

grief can serve as an opening to deep experience of God. It would take me much too far afield to explore that terrain in any detail.

Notes to Chapter 2

1. In October 2004, after varied ministry venues in Texas, he came up to Dallas to record an account of his experience with a Christian broadcasting company. On the night before the scheduled interview, he died of a heart attack in his hotel room. His wife was reported to have asked the medical establishment to make sure he was really dead. She did not want a repeat performance of what had happened before.

2. Pim van Lommel, *Consciousness beyond Life: The Science of Near-Death Experience* (New York: HarperCollins, 2010), 327.

3. Van Lommel, *Consciousness beyond Life*, 33.

4. Michael J. Gehring, *The Oxbridge Evangelist: Motivations, Practices, and Legacy of C. S. Lewis* (Eugene, OR: Cascade, 2017), 71.

Notes to Chapter 3

1. At this point I draw on the formal analysis developed in "Hope with a small 'h'," in *Hope*, ed. Ingolf U. Dalferth and Marlene A. Block (Tübingen: Mohr Siebeck, 2015).

2. In what follows I have benefited greatly from a critical engagement with J. P. Day, "Hope," *American Philosophical Analysis* 6 (1969): 89–102.

3. J. Cottingham, R. Stoothoff, and D. Murdoch, eds., *The Philosophical Writings of Descartes*, vol. 1 (Cambridge: Cambridge University Press, 1985), 289–90.

4. The crucial complication I have in mind is the gap between God's knowledge of the future and my claim to have access to God's knowledge of the future. Another way to express the complication is to draw attention to the necessity of God getting the future right when God knows the future and any contingent claim to have rightly identified what God has revealed about the future.

5. Symeon the New Theologian, *The Discourses* (Mahwah, NJ: Paulist Press, 1980), 160.

6. C. S. Lewis, "The Weight of Glory," in *They Asked for a Paper* (London: Geoffrey Bles, 1962), 204. Lewis notes how offensive he found this language initially.

7. The same dilemma shows up in attempts to describe cosmic eschatology.

8. Teresa of Avila, *The Collected Works of Teresa of Avila* (Washington, DC: ICS Publications, 1987), 1:232.

9. Quoted in Randy Alcorn, *Eternal Perspectives: A Collection of Perspectives on Heaven, the New Earth, and Life After Death* (Carol Stream, IL: Tyndale House, 2012), 16.

Notes to Chapter 4

1. Eleonore Stump, *Wandering in Darkness: Narrative and the Problem of Suffering* (Oxford: Oxford University Press, 2012), 184.

2. Stump, *Wandering in Darkness*, 223.

3. C. S. Lewis, "The Weight of Glory," in *They Asked for a Paper* (London: Geoffrey Bles, 1962), 205–6.

Notes to Chapter 5

1. Marilyn McCord Adams, *Christ and Horrors: The Coherence of Christology* (Cambridge: Cambridge University Press, 2006).

2. Adams, *Christ and Horrors*, 43; emphasis as in the original.

3. Adams, *Christ and Horrors*, 191; emphasis as in the original.

4. David Bentley Hart, *The Doors of the Sea: Where Was God in the Tsunami?* (Grand Rapids: Eerdmans, 2005).

5. Alexander Schmemann, *O Death, Where Is Thy Sting?* (Crestwood, NY: St. Vladimir's Seminary Press, 2003).

6. Hart, *The Doors of the Sea*, 13. Hereafter, page references to this work are given in parentheses in the text.

7. John Wesley, "The New Birth," in *The Works of John Wesley*, ed. Albert Outler (Nashville: Abingdon, 1985), 2:190.

Index of Names and Subjects

Index of Scripture References